CHILD-FREE ZONE

why more people are choosing NOT to be parents

Susan J. & David L. Moore

Child-Free, a division of Chequered Gecko Pty Ltd.
2 Larmer Place
Dee Why
NSW 2099
Australia
Telephone: +61 2 9981 7636
Facsimile: +61 2 9984 0144

Moore, Susan and David
Child-Free Zone: why more people are choosing not to be parents
ISBN 0-646-39494-0

Cover photographs by

John Doughty - Spy Photography
PO Box 58
Drummoyne
NSW 2047
Telephone: +61 2 9319 6199
Facsimile: +61 2 9319 2166
john@spyphotography.com.au

Cover design and Child-Free logo concept by Susan J. & David L.
Moore

3D Child-Free logo realised by Richard Salter

CHILD-FREE ZONE

why more people are choosing NOT to be parents

Susan J. & David L. Moore

Published by Chequered Gecko Pty Ltd

What people have said in anticipation of CHILD-FREE ZONE

'What an interesting topic to bring to the people...I know my friends and I will have many dinner party discussions about this one.' – Anne

'Ten points for your book idea, as I think there is a real need for Aussie literature in this area...' – Louise

'First of all, congratulations on being (possibly) the pioneer of endorsing what may be the most appropriate decision for so many people and for taking a stand against an infringement of your "right not to". Best of luck with the book.' – Kirk

'My congratulations to you on tackling this ever-so-important bioethical issue.' – Sally

'I must say you piqued my interest...my wife and I just separated over the issue. If you would like me to complete your questionnaire I would be more than happy. Maybe it [will] help me answer some of my own questions.' – Chris

'It was very reassuring to realise that I am not alone in my "selfish" decision not to bring more children into the world. I am looking forward to reading the book once it is published. Good luck!!' – Raquel

'I'm glad you're writing a book on this subject. We'll be eagerly awaiting its release.' – Samantha and Simon

'I listened with real interest to your segment on Triple J. It is a relief to be able to express these opinions without someone looking at you as though you are a weirdo or the worst person in the world, or telling you that some people would give anything to be able to have children blah blah blah.' – Marianne

'Thanks for pursuing a much needed subject!' – Rosemary

CONTENTS

Susan J. & David L. Moore

Introduction

Walk into any almost any bookstore in Australia and you will find a wealth of information about parenthood. From guides to pregnancy and 'baby's first year' to 'how to' child-rearing manuals, books about combining career and motherhood and books for New Age dads – there is no shortage of discussion on the subject of parenthood. Yet you'll be struggling to find even a passing mention of the alternative – *not* having children. It's as if there is no choice, that parenthood is so totally expected that it is beyond question. The thing is, these days we do have a choice, and the trend is for Australians to have fewer children, later in life, and for many not to have children at all. In the past, almost all couples who could do so had children, but today, many choose not to.

It's almost a taboo subject. When we started our research and told people about the subject matter, we received an interesting range of responses. At the mere mention of the subject, a number of parents felt that we were attacking them personally and denigrating their life choices. We also received a surprisingly large amount of positive, supportive feedback from parents and non-parents alike.

On digging deeper through libraries and online catalogues we came across a number of wonderful books on the topic of remaining childless by choice. Most of these were academic studies. The only 'popular press' Australian book on the topic presented what we thought was flawed or biased research; it contained interviews with a small group of single people who were missing the important ingredient for creating a child in the first place – a partner. Others who were interviewed were happy to be childless at the time, but felt that if the right partner came along and the time was right, they would reconsider. These people do not fit into our definition of 'voluntarily childless'. Most of the interviewees were employed in the arts, travel and media industries, where you would expect to find more child-free people due to the nature of the work. In this book we use the term 'child-free', as 'childless' implies a lack of something.

1

CHILD-FREE ZONE

Despite the stereotypes, the child-free in Australia fall into all categories. They are married or living de facto, divorced, single, young, old, heterosexual, gay or lesbian, white and blue collar workers, professionals and small business people. The only essential characteristic of the people we have interviewed is that they have made a conscious decision not to have children and are quite definite in that decision. However, we'd love to do a *7 Up* and revisit some of the younger ones in the future to see if the decision holds. When we were interviewed on radio station 702 ABC Sydney (formerly 2BL) during the research phase, presenter James Valentine asked the obvious question: 'This has been quite a public declaration on your behalf. What happens if you change your mind?' The answer, while facetious, was: 'That will be the next book, James.'

People who are *unable* to have children are a very different group to those who have chosen not to have them. Their experiences range from mild disappointment to extreme desperation and, although some decide to enjoy their life without children, many will try almost anything to have a family. As their experience is so different to those who have chosen to be child-free, and as there is ample literature on the subject, we have not covered this group of childless people. We have focused on those people who have made a positive decision not to be parents.

The comments in this book have been taken from questionnaires completed by more than 80 child-free people all over Australia, aged between 22 and 66. They come from a range of backgrounds and from different sized families, and live in regional and city areas. Their occupations include: clerk, nanny, ranger, hotel manager, sales assistant, psychologist, marketing manager, artist, solicitor, hairdresser, computer consultant, secretary, accountant, truck driver, make-up artist, doctor, police officer, teacher, flight attendant and registered nurse. There were also a number of self-employed and retired people surveyed. While such a small sample is not representative, and as a result we have not analysed the results statistically, we have attempted to cover a broad range of child-free Australians.

Susan J. & David L. Moore

Some of the opinions expressed by our survey respondents may be seen as extreme, and may even offend some people. We felt it was important to take the risk of offending people to give child-free people a voice. Many feel that they are unable to say what they think because is not socially acceptable, for example, that you don't like children or you think that people are 'breeding' rather than making an informed decision to have a family. So we hope you'll keep an open mind and enjoy the stories they have to tell.

We want to provide an insight into the lives of people who choose not to have children. Why don't they want to be parents? What are the pressures and prejudices they face? What do they do and what do they plan to do with their lives? And what are the benefits? Have they ever regretted their choice? Where are the child-free zones for recreation and holidays? Who are the role models for people making the decision now and what can they expect for their futures?

This book is also an attempt to address the imbalance in the discussion of parenthood. As one of our survey respondents, Anthea, said: '...the contemporary promotion of a culture around pregnancy, childbirth and motherhood has far outweighed the promotion of an aware, informed and intelligent acceptance of the decision not to bring more babies into the world.' Sometimes it is smart not to have children. And it's okay to talk about it.

We hope that as a result of this book more people like ourselves will look forward to a wonderful child-free future.

Facts and figures

Australians are marrying later, starting a family later in life and having fewer children.

Based on 1996 fertility rates, 75.1% of all women can expect to have at least one child in their lives and 58.2% will have at least two, 16.9% will have only one child, and 24.9% of women will remain childless. Since the mid-1980s approximately one in four women has remained childless.

That's almost a quarter of Australian women now of child-bearing age who are expected to remain childless. People are often surprised when confronted with these figures. But the number of childless women is growing: some sources now suggest that up to 29% of women will not be mothers. While it's impossible to break the percentage down into those who are unable to have children and those who choose not to, the rapid increase in the number of childless women since the early 1970s tells us that more than natural forces are at play.

Number of children that women bear

Years	No children	One child	Two children	Three children	More than three children
1985 to 1991	25.3%	13.6%	27.4%	11.5%	37.3%
1980 to 1984	23.7%	2.6%	32.6%	19.3%	23.8%
1975 to 1979	21.8%	9.2%	28.8%	18.2%	20.2%
1970 to 1974	10.3%	10.2%	29.5%	15.1%	19.9%

Source: Australian Bureau of Statistics, 1996.

Susan J. & David L. Moore

Based on data from the 1986 Census, 18.3% of women born in 1909 did not have children. They were 25 years old in the middle of the Great Depression. In comparison, of women born in 1936 who were 25 at the peak of the 'baby boom', only 8.6% did not have children. This is called 'generational fertility' and can only be calculated accurately after women have completed child-bearing at the age of about 50. It can be calculated for women born after 1965, as shown in the table above, using the projected age specific birthrates but is unreliable.

In *Australia in Facts and Figures* (1994) Bill Coppell points out that the number of women having babies in the 20 to 24 and 25 to 29 age groups has dropped considerably, while the birthrates for women aged 30 to 34 and 35 to 39 has increased. Couples now tend to start a family later in life, and the delay often becomes the reason they choose not to have children at all. The decision is delayed until suddenly they realise they are no longer able to have children, or that their lives are full and happy without them. Age specific birthrates – the number of live births registered in one year according to the age of the mother, per 1000 females of the same age – also reflect changing attitudes to child-bearing. In 1964, peak fertility was among 24-year-old women, with 23% having babies. By 1994, peak fertility was among 29-year-old women, but only 13% had babies.

In the late 1950s the average duration of marriage before the first pregnancy was 1.3 years. By 1990 this had increased to 2.3 years. It is taking longer to become established as a young family. Today, the duration of marriages is also having an effect on people's decision to stay childless. It is increasingly common for marriages to end in divorce, and some people are concerned that they may not be able to provide a stable future for a family.

Australia's fertility rate ranks equal fourteenth lowest in the world, part of a worldwide phenomenon that is particularly noticeable in developed nations. It peaked at 3.5 children per woman in 1961 during the 'baby boom' period and, by 1996, the fertility rate had fallen to 1.8. The population replacement level is 2.1 children per

5

woman, and Australia's fertility rate has been below that since 1976. This has not been attributed to improvements in contraception, rather linked to the increasing participation of women in the workforce and changing attitudes to family size, standards of living and lifestyle choices.

Fertility varies between states, regions and even suburbs. The Northern Territory has had consistently higher fertility rates than other states, and the ACT has the lowest fertility rate. Within capital cities, the inner city suburbs have the lowest fertility rates. In 1994 Central Melbourne and the eastern suburbs area of Sydney had the lowest fertility rates with 1.1 and 1.2, respectively, indicating that people who have chosen a life without children often live in the inner city. Conversely, people in the outer and fringe suburbs either choose to have more children or move there to give their growing families more space.

An increasing number of people are becoming alarmist about the fall in the birthrate. In an article by Felicity Dargan in Melbourne's *Herald-Sun* in 1998, Mary Helen Woods from the Family Planning Association said 'plunging birthrates are a sign that we no longer live in an altruistic society. Selfishness and hedonism have taken over'. A Liberal member of parliament in Victoria made it part of her political agenda, urging 'selfish career women' to become mothers to reverse the plummeting birthrate. Even the then Victorian Premier Jeff Kennett was heard at a Melbourne school in 1999 encouraging teenage girls to breed to halt the declining population. The arguments are always more emotional than rational, and based in a long-rooted history of 'blaming' someone for the decline in the birthrate.

However, despite low fertility rates, latest estimates say that Australia's population is growing at the world average of 1.3% a year, which is far higher than most other developed countries and even higher than South-East Asian nations such as Thailand. It is only 0.2% behind Indonesia which, with more than 216 million people, is the fourth most populous nation in the world. Australia's population growth rate is 50% higher than that of the US and more than six times the rate in the UK. In the US, the population is growing by much greater numbers, but by a smaller percentage of just 0.8% per year. Australia's population, which continues to grow through the immigration program and through increased life expectancy, reached 19 million in September 1999 and will hit 24.9 million by 2050 if neither migration nor the birthrate fall.

The lobby group, Australians for an Ecologically Sustainable Population, aims to encourage informed public debate about how population numbers affect the need to preserve Australia's ecological heritage. Its membership information claims that:

• In the last 50 years as much land was cleared as in the 150 years before 1945.

• Because our birthrate is twice our death rate we are locked into a population increase of two million before our population stabilises – even if there were no immigration at all. Current levels of immigration, plus natural increase, will see our population continue to grow.

• Decisions about population are political decisions. Our population will reach 20.7 million before it can stabilise, but it doesn't have to reach 27 million and still be growing by 2051.

American political humourist P.J. O'Rourke outlines an alternative account of the 'overpopulation problem' in his book *All the Trouble in the World*. He does a series of rough calculations and works out that the world is not really overpopulated at all. World fertility rates peaked a while ago and, even in the poorest countries, fertility rates dropped 30% between the late 1960s and the early 1980s. If this trend continues, world population growth could reach replacement level by 2005, when the UN estimates there will be 6.7 billion people. At the current population level, O'Rourke says, we could all live in Europe in a California-style suburban sprawl with 2250 people per square mile, with most of Russia west of the Urals left over for landfill. He says: 'This leaves us with the question of what people really mean when they say the world is overpopulated. What these concerned citizens usually mean is that they've seen a whole bunch of the earth's very ordinary people up real close, and the concerned citizens didn't like what they saw one bit.'

This is probably true: a quick trip to the local shopping centre is sometimes all you need to confirm that having more children is not going to help the world.

Statistics can always be used to prove different points. The facts are that the world population is still ballooning, the world's resources are finite and increasingly stretched, and an increasing number of Australians are choosing not to have children.

An historical perspective

In the mid-nineteenth century it was normal for married women in Australia to produce six or seven children. By the turn of the century the average had dropped to three or four. There was such widespread concern over the declining birthrate that, in 1903, a Royal Commission On the Decline in the Birth-rate and On the Mortality of Infants was instigated in NSW. In 1904 the Royal Commissioner reported that 'the cause or causes of the Decline of the Birthrate must be a force or forces over which the people themselves have control...' – in other words, even then, people were deliberately limiting the size of their families.

The blame apparently lay with women, who exhibited 'an unwillingness to submit to the strain and worry of children; a dislike of the interference with pleasure and comfort involved in child-bearing and child-rearing; a desire to avoid the actual physical discomfort of gestation, parturition and lactation; and a love of luxury and social pleasures'. When motherhood is described in those terms, can you blame women for not wanting to be a part of it?

In her book *Love and Freedom – Professional women and the reshaping of personal life* (1997), Alison Mackinnon points out how odd it is that women were blamed for the declining birthrate, when the primary method used by middle class couples to avoid pregnancy was withdrawal or coitus interruptus, which of course requires cooperation from the male. Mackinnon reports that the Royal Commission rejected a vast amount of evidence that showed couples simply could not afford more children.

Early this century, Australian women were admitted to universities and could vote in federal elections. Among educated women there was a growing belief that fewer children who were well loved and cared for, were better than many children with less chance of a happy and healthy life. Working class women were also having fewer children, but financial hardship was more likely to be the motivating factor.

In the 1950s couples could afford to live on one income. It was often still expected that a woman would cease employment once she was married. There was also a post-World War II swing against women working outside the home as they had become so independent during the war. Many women had to fight to retain the right to work, when male bosses encouraged them to become homemakers.

Survey respondent Jan, a registered nurse, was married in 1962, at the age of 21. While she never felt pressure from her own family to have children ('my mother asked once when she was to be a grandmother and was given the reply "never"; so the subject was not discussed again'), it was unusual and less acceptable for couples to choose the child-free path.

'These were times when it was generally expected [that] women married young, rarely travelled before marriage and were not independent in financial matters,' said Jan. 'They did not own their own cars or houses and mostly lived at home with their parents until marriage. Rarely did women have university degrees, most left school as soon as they reached 15 and worked in what was perceived as "female" positions. The assumption was that they would get married, produce children and stay at home to be a mother and so a tertiary education was not considered important unless one came from a family of professionals.

'It was generally expected that after a few years of marriage, children would eventuate. Contraception was a hit and miss affair, with diaphragms, condoms and the rhythm method to name a few, and many unplanned pregnancies occurred. The Pill was coming into vogue permitting some degree of choice in planning a family. Still it was unusual for a couple not to reproduce, and stranger still that they would choose not to have children.

'After we had been married for about four years, I had one well-meaning lady who knew there were no children on the scene pat me on the arm and whisper, "Never mind dear, you can always adopt." She could not understand when I explained we had chosen not to have children. Her generation had little choice, although in the 1960s, it was still expected for couples to follow the "norm". Couples today do make decisions not to have children and up to a point, their decisions are more accepted than in the 1960s.'

Despite the rapid change in social attitudes in the last three decades, anecdotal evidence tells us that there is still a widespread expectation that couples should become parents.

A matter of choice

The overwhelming concern of child-free people is that they have a right to choose without their choice constantly being questioned. They would like others to respect their decision. It is no different to choosing where to live, with whom you live and what you do in your spare time. Unlike having children, staying child-free rarely interferes with other people's lives and should be of no concern to anyone other than the person who has made that choice.

'I find your particular reasons for your decision not to [have children] most reasonable,' wrote Kirk, 28, following a radio interview conducted during the writing of this book. 'The fact that you do not find children an attractive option, among other reasons, is your own belief and decision; a right that is yours and yours only; a right that should not be open to criticism or argument. It doesn't matter whether this "right not to" is to do with not accepting responsibility, or because you'd rather save for a holiday, or you'd rather adopt a homeless child, or just because you don't like children.'

Child-free people are tired of other people not taking their decision seriously. When you tell others that you don't want children the usual response is 'you'll change your mind'. Parenthood is still seen as inevitable for anyone who marries, so some people choose to remain single or live de facto as this reduces the pressure from family to reproduce.

Jacqui, 25, says she is sick of 'answering the same silly, intrusive question over and over. Why are people so fascinated that we are choosing to go against the grain on this issue?'

'One thing I would like to see change is people's insistence that they have a right to convert me to their way of thinking on this issue,' wrote Monica, 30. 'I have a horse…which I gain a great deal of joy from but I don't insist that everyone else should love them and do the same. I realise people are different and that what is right for some is not for others.'

'Over the years, I have done my fair share of defending myself to others with kids, which to me is strange because I have never demanded to know their justification for having children,' said Julie, 37. The point is that people don't have to justify having children. Humans have been reproducing for millions of years. It is only recently that we have been able to think about it and choose.

People are now presented with an almost limitless array of options in their lives. You could fill a dozen life spans with recreational activities alone. The boundless opportunities often seem to catch active people out. They are simply too busy living life to be bothered having children or even think of it in time.

It is obvious that non-parents simply cannot know what it is like to have a child, so it is slightly insulting when parents claim they somehow know 'better' than you and imply that you are ignorant of the joy that children can bring. Of course we don't know. But we have some idea, and have chosen not to experience it. As Erica, 34, puts it: 'I often get the comments: "Oh but Erica it's different when they're your own" and "it's something every woman should experience". Bollocks. Some women are meant to be managing directors of multimillion dollar corporations, some women are meant to be sprinters, some women are meant to be electricians and some women are meant to have children and some aren't.'

It's simply about exercising the right to choose and then not being judged on that choice for the rest of your life.

Why do people choose to be child-free?

Having children is an enormous undertaking. There are so many things to think about, so many things you can't predict, so many things that you can't guarantee, so much to learn, so much to do, such a long-term commitment and, at the end of it all, you have to let them go. Any one of these things can become a compelling reason not to have children if you feel strongly enough about it.

When people who have raised children find out what our book is about they sometimes say 'Oh God, I can tell you why not to' or 'Ask my husband, he'd never do it again' or 'Whatever you do, don't change your mind'. A more common response is: 'I love my children dearly and would not give them up for anything in the world, but if I had my time again, knowing what I know now, I would not have kids.'

When people with young children find out that you don't want any, they almost invariably try to change your mind. One theory is that misery loves company. The conspiracy of parenthood dictates that those who are now bound by their decision must attempt to recruit more victims to the fold. It is like a 'baby cult'. You believe because you have to believe. It is too late to admit it was a mistake even if it was. You are now bound to spend a quarter of your life on this project. You can't even allow the thought that you might have been wrong to enter your head. The conspiracy of silence about parenthood means that many new parents are left asking 'Why didn't anyone tell me how hard this would be?' In popular culture, parenthood is romanticised and glorified when, for many, the reality is different. It takes a lot of guts to admit it.

Those who have finished raising their children are in a position to reflect more objectively, and sometimes that reflection is not as pretty as they once thought. That objectivity, combined with experience, is difficult to ignore. Some child-free people feel that they have simply learned from other people's mistakes and listened to their advice.

Susan J. & David L. Moore

The people we surveyed gave a wide variety of responses when asked why they don't want children. Most people who have decided not to have a family will see themselves reflected somewhere in this chapter.

Many respondents said they simply had not found a good reason *to* have children. Says Marianne, 31, a graphic designer: 'I can't relate to other people's reasons for *wanting* to have kids. Children are often so idealised and inevitably parents realise this not long after the child is born when the barrage of nappies and crying hits. It's all worthwhile, they tell me. Is it?'

'I never actually decided *to* have children,' wrote Stephanie, 36, who has five brothers and two sisters. 'Coming from a large family there were always too many children about. Being the youngest I was always surrounded by too many nieces and nephews.'

Helen, 33, says that having children would affect her life 'very badly. I don't like children, I don't want children, it just wouldn't work for me,' she said. 'I don't mean to sound melodramatic, but it would ruin my life.'

Not all child-free people dislike children, in fact many are closely involved with children in their work and family lives, but so often children are 'their own worst enemy'. Put simply, the perceived decline in standards of behaviour of 'children today' puts many people off having them. Even with the best of them it is not long before your tolerance is tested. So would you want one of your own full time? 'Ah, but mine would be different!' you might say. How do you know?

Tracey, 39, considers herself truly child-free by choice, although she has had a baby. 'I relinquished a child for adoption at 16, and have never had the desire for children since, or before for that matter. I don't consider myself a mother and never have. I wanted to be free of responsibility at 16, and still want to be free. I may not be considered a "child-free person" as I've had a baby. Then again, you could view it another way. If one has a child, or even falls pregnant, and then gives that child up, or has an abortion, one would truly be child-free by choice. I mean, once you already have that child, or are pregnant with it, then you have to have the courage of your convictions in making the decision to stay child-free.'

Child-free people are sometimes perceived as child haters. Yet to care so much for a child as to give it up for a better home, or not have the child all, may be the single most thoughtful and caring thing a person may ever do for a child. It is obvious they aren't child haters when they think of a child's welfare that far in advance. Prevention is better than cure.

This concern may initially manifest itself as doubt. 'I don't know if I want to bring a child into a world like this.' 'I don't know if I could be a good parent.' Don't just ask yourself these questions. Answer them, and answer them before you have a child, because afterwards your answer doesn't matter.

Greater freedom

An overwhelming majority of respondents mentioned 'freedom', as either a key reason not to have children or the main benefit of staying child-free.

'My situation is rather paradoxical, as you will see. I just love children of all ages, and I think the world would be a very sad place without them. However I must confess that I love my freedom more, hence my choice of a child-free life,' said Vivienne, 59.

'I value my freedom and independence very highly,' said Monica, 30. 'I like to be able to get in my car and go somewhere without first loading it with the large amount of necessary accessories that go with children, or having to make alternative arrangements for childcare.'

Tracie, 35, says she is not prepared to give up her independence. 'I like the freedom to do what I want when I want. I also feel a child would interfere in my partner's and my lifestyle and we spend a lot of time by ourselves.'

'Our lifestyle is very important to us,' said Stephanie, a 36-year-old sales assistant. 'We have always put each other first. We prefer to be around animals and enjoy coming home to a quiet house with no children running around.'

The second most important reason Betty, 47, chose not to have children was lifestyle. 'It was around 1970 I read an excerpt from a book called The Baby Trap in *Cosmopolitan* of all magazines. The author was celebrating her child-free honeymoon in Europe which she said was possible because they weren't tied down with children. I read the book and it wasn't particularly well written but it raised a lot of valid points.'

'I have always been happy the way I am, and having a child would make me very unhappy indeed – anxious, trapped and unable to please myself,' said Fiona, 41. 'Having a child would reduce my choices and opportunities for work, fun, lifestyle and happiness. I think that's why people say they find happiness and fulfilment in their children – they don't have the time or energy to find it elsewhere. There's also the risk of being locked into a situation that's second rate, for security's sake.'

'I feel that all my life I have been doing things to please others, but not necessarily what I wanted to do,' said Beth, 34. 'This decision is right for me and I guess others might view it as selfish but I don't want to lose the freedom I currently have.'

Mik, 41, said that not having kids means he has 'freedom to do as, when and for what I like, without responsibility.'

Freedom is whatever you perceive it to be. For some, it means being able to 'up stumps' and move at a moment's notice. For others it means having as few obligations as possible. Some people see leaving the workforce to become a full-time parent as a form of freedom. After all, many people would love to give up working.

However, parenting can be far more arduous than almost any job and it doesn't offer the luxury of being able to seek a career change when you're tired of it.

Already part of a large family

Only three out of the 80 people surveyed were only children. A surprising number of respondents came from large families and felt they had done their fair share of 'parenting' or had enough children in their lives.

'I was the eldest of 11 children and as such a version of a mother,' said Theresa, 42. 'Mothers have the maturity to appreciate a child's development, therefore making the work associated with child-rearing pleasant and enjoyable. As a child I was not capable of this type of appreciation – I only recognised the work. It just seems like work to me.'

Helen, 33, is the youngest of nine children and being a parent is something she has 'always known' she didn't want to do. 'There were grandchildren on the scene from when I was six years old. Four out of the nine have chosen to be child-free. So I received no pressure from my family,' she said.

Women with partners who have children from a previous marriage may also decide that there are enough children in their lives. Raising and disciplining someone else's child can be fraught with difficulties.

'I have only recently made this decision not to have children,' said Heather, 32. 'My husband has three children, now adults aged 22, 20 and 18, whom I helped raise from when the eldest son was 10 years of age. I've been through and am still going through teenage years and feel that although I love the kids I don't wish to go through "all that" again. My stepdaughter has a seven-month-old son and my husband and I have quite a bit to do with him. I really enjoy these times and sometimes feel that I can enjoy him as if he were my own. However, it was primarily my own personal decision [not to have children] as my hubby was happy for us to have children.'

Aware of the responsibility

'Working with kids soon made me realise what a big responsibility they are,' said Anaïs, 38, who runs her own nanny agency.

Handling other people's children can quickly instil a sense of the responsibilities associated with parenting. Some child-free people even express a fear of being left alone with other people's children, and most of all hate having babies thrust into their arms.

'I was once conned into an outing to an amusement park where children were going to be in my care,' said Dave, 32. 'If I had known this beforehand, I would not have taken part. During the course of the day, one of the children started misbehaving. She was doing all sorts of annoying and naughty things. I asked her to stop on several occasions, explaining why. I then told her that the next incident would involve a punishment and that I was serious. Of course this was like a red rag to a bull – my inexperience showing through perhaps – and the girl immediately continued to destroy some of my belongings. So I said "stop it" and squeezed her hand to let her know that I meant business. Eventually she burst into tears just as my friend returned from another ride. When he saw the child crying the accusations and the looks I got were quite unbelievable. The little girl lied to him, of course, and yet it was still my word against hers and suddenly I looked like a child beater. If she had been my child she would have been smacked after the first warning.'

'I've never even owned a pet,' said Roger, 35. 'Plants die in my care. I don't feel like washing my car. When I get home from work, I like to relax or just go, without much of a plan. I like the fact that when I leave work, I have virtually no other responsibilities, other than to be a good husband. I could handle the responsibility, I just prefer not to.'

CHILD-FREE ZONE

Lorraine, 52, said that she was put off children by 'the thought that I could actually be a huge influence on another human being. I did not want that responsibility'.

'[Having a child is] a lifetime commitment with no guarantees,' said Louise, 32.

'The responsibility would be unbearable for me,' said Gabby, 32. 'My freedom would be snatched away from me and I would be on Prozac for the rest of my life. I'm highly strung enough without children so I'd end up being a bundle of nerves and muscle twitches on legs. Not only would a child not be good for me but I wouldn't be good for a child.'

You've probably heard of American children who are now suing their parents for the way they were raised. All sorts of parenting decisions are now being flung back at the parents in the form of lawsuits. Repressed memory analysis is even bringing up stuff that didn't occur. Perhaps you should even be worried if you once donated sperm or ova?

'If I had a child I would be living for someone else,' said Tracie, 35. 'It's not that I'm selfish, I just don't want to be that responsible.'

We must be careful how we bundle 'responsibility' and 'responsible' together in this context. The desire to avoid 'responsibility' has led these survey respondents to make a 'responsible' decision. Being aware of your own shortcomings, if that is what they are, allows you to factor them into your decisions and prevent them from becoming a problem.

Knowing that children are a big responsibility has its drawbacks when you talk to parents. More often than not, their response to your acknowledgement of the size of the responsibility is to point out that 'You'd make great parents because you're sensible and you know it is a big job.' On the contrary – child-free people have been responsible enough to know what a huge responsibility it is to have children and smart enough to live by that knowledge.

Susan J. & David L. Moore

Career opportunities

It seems obvious that those without children generally have more time and energy to focus on work. However, while career or business aspirations featured heavily in the surveys received, most emphasised career flexibility rather than scaling the heights of the corporate world. Some felt strongly that they would be unable to achieve to the same level if they had children. Changing jobs and careers is a feature of the modern workforce, and child-free people have more flexibility to adapt to this new order.

Vicki, 32, and her husband are self-employed tradespeople, and don't like the 9-to-5 routine. 'We don't have to work as hard as we would if we had children,' said Vicki. 'We see a lot of friends really start to struggle financially when they have a family. The husbands seem to have to work so much that they never see the child anyway. We're not too financially well off, but we're comfy for two.'

There was a time not so long ago when a couple could afford to have one at work, usually the male, and one at home raising the kids. Many parents did this and ended up doing just fine in the long run. However, these days it is rarely enough to have one person in a couple working. They would hardly be able to provide food and shelter for themselves, let alone a third person.

Roger enjoys the flexibility in selecting jobs and locations, and moved to Australia in 1997 with his (then) new wife simply because they could. 'We're not slaves to work,' he said. 'We only have to prepare for our retirement, not worry about university and so on. I have a theory that some parents work hard, then feel guilty about not spending enough time with their kids, so they work even harder to afford more things for their kids to make up for not spending time with them, which makes them feel more guilty.'

People with careers that involve a lot of travel or a high degree of uncertainty and risk find it easier not to have children. They include actors, journalists, airline stewards and musicians.

People are being encouraged to work from home, start a small business or freelance. If you have kids it is harder to choose one of these options. Being child-free gives you the freedom to adopt new ways of working.

To make a better family

People who did not enjoy their childhood are often unwilling to risk 'inflicting' the same trauma on another human being, and decide not to bring a child of their own into the world.

Eight per cent of marriages now end in divorce within five years, 19% within ten years and 32% within 20 years. In 1991, 54.2% of divorces involved children (Bill Coppell, 1994). That leaves a lot of kids who have been affected by it. The chances of ending up on your own with a child also appears to be growing.

'Our decision is partly a result of our own childhoods,' wrote Christine, 39. 'Both were equally "loveless" and both ended in divorce.'

G.H., 42, said that 'unstable relationships' were her primary reason for not having children. 'I am convinced that it needs two people to support each other in the child-rearing process,' she said.

'I did not see [having children] as a fulfilling life for my own mother,' said Lyndall, 47. 'All she did was work very hard for very little thanks. I saw her as a martyr. It didn't seem fair to "inflict" life on an innocent child for my own social or narcissistic reasons. I did not have a happy childhood or young adulthood.'

'My mother never hid from her children the fact that they were unwanted and that she would have been better off without them,' said Sarah, 37. 'Knowing the pain that this has caused me, I would never, ever, bring a child into the world [who] wasn't wanted. I get so angry when people say I'm selfish for not having a child. Surely it's selfish to have a child just because society or your religion demands it or expects it of you.'

'My childhood was not wholly pleasant – much of it was "taken" from me,' said Gayle, a 36-year-old psychologist. 'I'm having my turn at being care and worry free as an adult. I would never want to burden anyone emotionally as I was by my mother and her circumstance.' Gayle also reports that due to her background, 'it is understood that I have made a considered and informed choice'.

'I knew when I was a teenage[r] I would never want children, perhaps because I was never exposed to any positive parent-child relationships,' said Lori, 42.

Louise, 42 and her partner Tony, 45, both felt that their own childhoods had affected their decision not to have a family. 'I hadn't had a very happy childhood and didn't want to pass on my negative feelings,' said Louise. Tony says he was influenced by 'the fact that I was not happy at school and did not get on with my father'.

Anne and her older sister have both chosen to be child-free. 'In discussions with my sister, we blame our grandmother who didn't like children, and passed on the feeling to her son, my father, who really only got on well with me once I'd turned 20 or so.'

A friend of ours has a theory as to why time flies as you get older. As Einstein said, time is relative. When you are five years old, a year is one-fifth of your life. Santa's next visit is a long time away. But when you are 30 a fifth of your life is six years. Although this is a simplistic view, it makes sense that events shared by parents and offspring seem far worse to the children. It's hardly surprising that someone who experienced divorce as a child is often not keen to reproduce.

A positive contribution to the environment

Whether as a primary or a secondary reason, issues such as overpopulation, crime, global unrest and conservation of the environment often play a part in the decision to remain child-free. Many child-free people feel that there are already enough people stretching the earth's resources and needing assistance, and that they have a responsibility to help the situation rather than bring more people into the world.

Kim, a veterinarian, said there are 'too many people in the world, not enough whales'. Kim and her husband sponsor a whale and have provided their parents, who were keen for grandchildren, with a photo of it as the 'grandchild'.

Marianne, 31, defined her concern about the world's chronic overpopulation problem as one of her main reasons for remaining childless. 'Why introduce another child into the world when people everywhere are pushing babies out at a ridiculous rate. I think the Catholic religion has a lot to answer for in their stance against contraception. The more people [who] are brought into the world, the harder stretched our natural resources become. Life is so cheap in other poorer countries.'

'In my mid-teens I read an article either written by or quoting Jacques Cousteau who said to ecologically sustain a Western middle class lifestyle for all, the global population should not exceed 400 million people,' said Betty, 47. 'In the 1970s, David Suzuki made a similar remark but said it should not exceed 200 million! This was the start of the decision making process to which a lot of other things contributed as I grew up. The first time I stated I would not have children, I believe I was 20. It was 1970 and not a lot of women were saying that.'

Betty said her main reason for choosing not to have a child was concern for the environment. 'I cannot remember the source of this quote but I believe it to be profoundly true – 'you can recycle, compost and car pool until the cows come home but the single most important thing you can do to make a contribution to the environment is not have a child.' The song by American folk singer Fred Small, "Too Many People (having too many babies)", summarises many of the reasons we decided against having children.'

Susan J. & David L. Moore

There's a growing backlash to consumerism. People wanting to simplify their lives and 'tread lightly' on the earth look to the growing landfills as evidence of the problems caused by a consumption and a growing population. It's a deciding factor for many people who choose not to have children. For others it is simply a convenient higher ground to take in the discussion on the pros and cons of parenting.

'Current social and environmental conditions are not conducive to having children,' said John, 42. 'Do we really want to bring another child into a world where thousands of children are dying every day, into an overpopulated world with an increasing crime rate, global warming and so on?'

Ana, 27, a psychologist and active environmentalist, also says that she does not want to 'compound the overpopulation problem and its many side effects'.

'I grew up with ZPG (zero population growth) in the 1960s while my peers were still dreaming about three or four kids,' wrote Kate, 55. 'I'm sure you're aware that even Australia has a population problem – from an ecological point of view, from an infrastructure and social perspective. Therefore, the likes of us are the responsible ones. We should be given a tax advantage for NOT further burdening society. But we know this isn't going to happen.'

Ros, 45, is a part-time Landcare coordinator and volunteer on many natural resource management committees. She cites planetary overpopulation by our species as her main reason for not having a child. 'I can nurture the planet and give my time to natural resource issues instead of offspring,' she said.

'The destruction of forests and national heritage areas like Kakadu makes me wonder what will be left for future generations,' said Nicole, 23.

Jan, 57, decided not to have children in the 1960s. 'I did not have a conscious problem with these issues,' she said. 'They were something that my husband considered. He feels strongly that kids don't ask to be born and this world is not always a great place to be.'

'I think there are enough children in the world without parents, and I'm not only talking babies here,' said Lyn, 44. 'I think it is selfish to have more children when there are so many already without homes. If I really wanted a child I'd adopt. I think it is selfish to bring kids into the world as it is. I have to wonder what is ahead for future generations in terms of a healthy environment in which to live. In terms of world economies and unemployment I feel it can't be guaranteed that future generations are going to be able to work and support themselves.'

'While we are not "childless", having adopted two little boys whilst living in the US twenty years ago, we felt very strongly that we should not bring more children into the world when there are so many unwanted ones already here,' said Eleanor. 'Our kids were 3 years old when we adopted them, in the so called difficult-to-place category. While I think we were young and naive going into the adoption process, and it has certainly not been easy, we feel that we have done the right thing by not further burdening society and the planet.'

Beth has a large family and a partner with two children from a previous marriage. It's perhaps not surprising that she believes there are more than enough children already. 'I have travelled quite a bit and spent time in Africa and Asia. Certainly there you get to see hardships we can't imagine, and yet there are always so many children. I feel that the world population can probably do with a few of us opting out of child-bearing. Given I am one of seven children, my mother has already "replaced" me, and I know my sisters will all have children so I don't feel compelled.'

A common attitude to so many problems seems to be 'I'll be dead by the time that happens, so why worry?'. This may be so, but why do we only use it for the negative things? We don't worry about pollution as much as we should because, chances are, we don't think it will become unbearable in our lifetimes. But many people think that if one of us decides not to have children the place will be empty before we die. 'If we don't replace ourselves the human race will disappear.' Don't laugh, we've heard it said. And, if so, why not apply the 'Well, I'll be dead before that happens' attitude to it?

Has GOOD WEEKEND been taken over by the so-called pro-lifers? First, those of us who choose not to breed were denigrated for 'eroding the population base that should pay for their pensions in their old age' ('Where have all the people gone?' January 17). Then, in 'Little Darlings' (January 31), China's eminently sensible one-child policy was described as 'draconian'.

We live on a horrendously polluted planet, yet this breed-at-any-cost mentality lives on. I am reminded of a wonderful quote I once read: 'You can compost, recycle, carpool … until the cows come home, and it won't compare to the environmental impact of bringing one less child into the world.'

Parents should be thanking us for leaving a cleaner planet for their offspring to inherit.

Letter to The Good Weekend, *February 1998*

Many child-free people say that while their decision has been largely based on personal reasons, they sometimes use environmental issues as justification or reinforcement of their decision.

'When I was younger I used these excuses to justify my decision to some extent,' said G.H., 42. 'However, I believe few people would let these things stop them if they really wanted to have kids.'

27

'Environmental factors do now have an effect on my decision because I travel extensively in Third World countries and see so many children entrenched in poverty and economic downfall,' said Janelle, a 33-year-old importer. 'But my decision not to breed was made long before I experienced this, so it only reinforced my decision.'

Global factors have not influenced Louise's decision to stay child-free. 'But they add to any high moral ground I choose to stand on when discussing the topic,' she said.

We've always found the annual 'Red Nose Day' fundraising event for sudden infant death syndrome (SIDS) in Australia to be a strange way of trying to help kids. On this day people buy red plastic noses by the thousand and wear them. Trucks and cars have larger versions attached to their grilles. Truck and car sized plastic noses are installed on buildings. This event has been going on for years and we can't help but feel that it is a short-sighted activity. Hopefully one of the children saved by all this plastic will be smart enough to come up with a way to clean it up at the end of the day. But in reality, this is just one small example of unnecessary pollution.

'Stop at two' may have been a radical concept when zero population growth was founded in 1968, but it was barely adequate even then. The replacement fertility level of 2.1 children per woman would not result in true zero population growth for many years. The notion that producing two descendants simply 'replaces' a couple is clearly wrong. We aren't salmon – we don't spawn and die. With increased life expectancy, many of us would be around to see our children beget, and those begotten beget to boot.

When a couple of us 'replace' ourselves, our environmental impact doubles. That's assuming our offspring's lifestyles are as environmentally friendly as ours, and that they won't replace themselves. Each of us in the industrialised world has a huge impact on nature. It is said that, in terms of energy consumption, when an Australian has two children it might be the same as an average East

Indian couple having 60, or an Ethiopian couple having 1000. It just doesn't add up.

Slightly tongue-in-cheek, the Voluntary Human Extinction Movement says that regardless of how many progeny we have or haven't produced to date, rather than stop at two, we must stop at once.

Towards a healthier population

If there is a chance that a person may bring an unhealthy child into the world, then that can be a reason for not having that child. This is clear from the points raised by the following survey respondents. However, there is more than the child's own life to consider. For many people the risk to their own health – physical and mental – is just too great.

'My mother died aged 49, when I was 12, of breast cancer,' said Laura, a 41-year-old doctor. 'Because I too have a high risk of developing breast cancer I didn't want to be in that position, especially since if I had had a child, it would have been in my late 30s. I have also had a period of depression in my life and I feared having post-natal depression.'

Kim, 40, said that a 'genetic tendency to mental illness' was one of the main reasons she has chosen not to have a child.

'Both my husband and I were sick a lot as kids, some of which could be passed on,' said Rachel, 37. 'We also don't want to go through the physical stress of pregnancy, birth and young child care. We are flat out trying to keep ourselves happy, let alone someone else.'

'After suffering from severe depression about four years ago I feel that I am not able to be, nor do I want to be, responsible for a child,' said Nicole, a 23-year-old student.

'Both my husband and I are cancer survivors – we feel [there] would be a possibility of passing it on,' said Lori, 42.

Anaïs, 38 said there have been a number of deaths in her family, including her mother's death from breast cancer eleven years ago. 'I'm worried that there might be something wrong with my child,' she said.

'Last year I was diagnosed with insulin dependant diabetes mellitus,' said Kim, 29, 'which makes having a healthy child more difficult. There would be health risks, at least during the pregnancy.'

Age and health were important factors for Vicki, 32, and her husband, who is seven years older. 'A lot of our friends have had sick children,' she said. 'My husband has already spent seven years of his life nursing a dying partner before he met me. We're not sure that we want to take the chance.'

'My wife has lower back problems which could be a problem in carrying a child,' said John, 42, 'although as I understand, this does not necessarily exclude the possibility of having one.'

Age was an important issue for William who was 40 when he married. 'External pressure was put upon my wife [by acquaintances] which forced us to confront the issue in a quiet and honest appraisal.' Now 53, William said, 'The health of my 42-year-old wife and her foetus would be a very great concern.'

We found out, well after our decision to be child-free, that there was history of a genetic disorder in our family. Cultural factors tended to mask the disabilities, which were often blamed on accidents, until a recurring theme became apparent.

Birth and beyond

Susan J. & David L. Moore

*And he said to the woman, 'I will increase your trouble in
pregnancy and your pain in giving birth. In spite of this,
you will still have desire for your husband, yet you will be
subject to him.'*

Genesis 3.16

Despite this frightening verse from the Bible, few survey
respondents mentioned fear of childbirth as a reason for not having
children. Helen, 33, is surprised that this would be a reason for
anyone not to have children. 'It amazes me that people think my
reason for not wanting children is that I must be afraid of the pain of
childbirth,' she said. 'I have had this response quite a lot, even from
a doctor. To my mind, childbirth is the easy part, it's the following
25 years I'm afraid of.'

Mum once said, when asked how you can go back to have a second
child after suffering through 36 hours of labour with the first, that
you 'just forget' the pain. We stared incredulously. How could you
'forget' such a momentous occasion and the pain that goes along
with it? Many women will admit to a fear of giving birth, and the
after-effects of birth, including post-natal depression. It is often a
fear of the unknown, with the code of silence upheld by generations
of mothers on the subject of childbirth and child-rearing, as
discussed in Susan Maushart's *The Mask of Motherhood*.

'The thought of the physical birth itself terrifies me,' said Jacqui,
25, 'and it's not an element which can be avoided.'

Jane, 48, said she has a fear of childbirth. 'I found it very
mechanised in Australia, while home births are very common in the
UK,' she said.

In an interview with ABC Radio National in October 1997,
urologist Dr Helen O'Connell, discussed the problem of
incontinence in women. She said that mild leakage, or occasional

episodes, occurs in up to 45%, even more, of women. Severe leakage is occurring in between 5% and 10% of the population. Childbirth is the number one risk factor. Instrumental delivery and any significant birth injury are the key causes. Physical and mental side effects may be seen as a reason to have children more often than childbirth itself.

"With my slightly depressive personality, I'm sure I would suffer from post-natal depression," said Amanda, 34. "I gain a lot of my self-esteem from my work and my sporting interests, and not being able to participate in these would really get me down. I'm more afraid of that than giving birth."

Lorraine, 52, said she was put off having children by 'the horror of childbirth itself'. She said she has 'always found the very thought of it verging on the obscene'.

Plenty of men have a fear of childbirth too. To do the right thing, they must be present during the birth. It is the very least they can do, apart from delivering the seed in the first place. However, many have absolutely no desire to be there. It might be the most emotional moment in your life, but not, perhaps, if you are squeamish and pale at the sight of blood.

To be in control

Some child-free people simply enjoy peace, quiet and order. They are not interested in anything that would spoil this for them.

Anne, a high school teacher, says her life would be 'totally upside down' if she'd had children. 'I have to admit I'm a Capricorn who likes to be in control,' she said. 'I'm a worrier and worrying about myself, my cats, my house, my job, my students, my friends and relatives takes up a lot of energy. A child would take up too much. I also suspect I wouldn't be able to avoid being a too controlling parent.'

Susan J. & David L. Moore

'I like organisation and everything to be clean and tidy, I have enough trouble keeping my partner in line,' said Maria, 23.

'I feel if I was to have children now, I would be resentful towards them for interfering with my life,' said Janelle, 33.

Children grow up thinking that everything revolves around them – largely because it does. They also believe that everything in the family home is theirs. It is not until later that they may realise that you only get what you earn. This inevitable loss of control at the material level and the more obvious loss of control at the individual level are something that some people just don't want to experience.

Dave, 32, said 'I remember once, shortly after getting my drivers license, asking my parents for a loan of the car. Notice I called it "the" car. The request was denied, as it had been on several, but not all, occasions before. I snapped on this occasion and said, "Why the hell can't I use the car? It is just sitting in the garage. It isn't going anywhere else." My parents' car, at that time, was a pretty good car. I now have a pretty good car and I can tell you that there is no way that I would let any teenager drive that car, even a child of my own.'

You also lose control when you don't know what is going on. Most people have done many things they wouldn't tell their mother. Your mother has probably guessed a lot of it, but even so, extrapolating what you have done and got away with on to a child of your own is a scary prospect. Kids have always got into trouble, but as we write this another high school massacre with an alarming number of automatic weapons and explosive devices has taken place in the US. You can't help but wonder when the first teenager will build a nuclear bomb from parts purchased on the Internet, and hope it won't be your child.

In the movie *Guess Who's Coming To Dinner*, a mixed race relationship quickly blossomed into an engagement and an impending wedding. A family dinner was the first time that parents on both sides were to discover that their child was marrying outside of their race. There was a particular scene where Sidney Poitier's character's father trotted out all the usual 'parent guilt trip' phrases. 'I have given you the best of everything, I have done this, I have done that, all for you', and so on. Sidney's response rang true – these aren't the exact words, but it was along the lines of: 'I did not ask to be born. That decision was yours. From that point on it was your obligation and duty to afford me every care and opportunity in life. You owed this to me. I owe you nothing.' Remember this when you think your kids will look after you in your old age.

To some degree, you always have control before something happens. After the event is too late. When you are child-free you can be more in control. Almost all parents talk of the freedom they'll enjoy when their children leave. Child-free people choose this freedom right from the start.

We just don't want to!

Few child-free people mention a dislike for children, but many claim they simply have 'no interest' in children.

Pauline, 55, said she just generally didn't want to have a child. 'When I was much younger I always thought I would have a family, but then I was a very religious person until I was 22, so that would have had an effect on that. I just never had any great inclination to, I did not see it as a positive thing to do. It would have been a very negative experience for me. I would have been irritated by the constant demands.'

Roger, 35 says he has simply no interest in procreating. 'I don't have a burning desire to be a parent, it's really that simple,' he said. 'I don't feel the need to conform to the societal norm and procreate because "that's what everyone else does" or "that's what's expected of me".'

Jan, 57, said that there were 'no maternal instincts at all' on her part. 'I disliked playing with dolls as a child and with babies as an adult,' she said. 'You cannot rely on this 'maternal feeling' occurring after the birth of a child.'

Kim, 40, says she has only a 'detached interest' in children. 'I'm never surprised when the child follows the normal growth curve, which is always a source of amazement to parents – the growth curve as well as our lack of amazement.'

'I didn't want any [children] and am appalled by the number of people who have them simply because they can,' said Anne. 'As a teacher, I have seen too many people's "mistakes" to believe I'd be clever enough to bring up a worthwhile child. So what's worthwhile, you ask. Yes, exactly.'

'It's similar to asking someone to try drugs for the first time,' said Mik, 41. 'It's simply an experience that I don't want.'

'There has always been tremendous social pressure for us to find small children appealing and I think this is why I feel so uncomfortable around them,' said Normajeane, 34. 'I don't like feeling guilty because I don't get a warm fuzzy feeling when I see a small child or a baby and I'm sick of pretending that I do.'

'While I don't like seeing or hearing of any child being abused, I'm just not interested,' said Tracey, 39. 'They don't thrill and delight me. I can't stand babies. If I see a woman with a pram, I feel sorry for her, she's got a ball and chain.'

Philippa, 41 says she has never felt 'driven or had desire to' have children. 'It's very easy to have a child, it's a difficult challenge not to have one in this society,' she said. Philippa listed 'global issues – too many of us' as her first reason for not having children.

'I like babies,' said Raquel, 27. 'I'm actually extremely good with babies. But anything older than 18 months either annoys or bores the crap out of me. Oh, and I only like babies if I can give them back...'

CHILD-FREE ZONE

> 'I don't like children,' said Monica, 30. 'One would almost think this was illegal judging by the reactions of people to this. I don't like olives, hot weather, country and western music or football either. But say you don't like children and people can't seem to accept it. There must be a scientific reason for this inability to understand such a simple concept but I don't know what it is. I do not find children cute or funny or amusing. For me they have no endearing characteristics and are best avoided or ignored.'

'Teenagers are OK,' said Kathryn, 43. 'Anyone younger than five and I have a problem! Babies scare me. I hate holding them.'

Many child-free people feel mild to extreme discomfort or even horror when parents insist on thrusting their offspring into their arms. Little girls in particular are always asked if they want to 'nurse the baby', as preparation for inevitable motherhood. One reaction that we have found effective is to hand the child straight back to them in one fluid motion. You can also try putting your hands behind your back and clasping them together, but you would be amazed how many parents still thrust the child at you and threaten to let go.

'I was never really comfortable around babies,' said Vicki, 32. 'To have someone else's new baby shoved into my arms to nurse just didn't feel right to me. I've changed that feeling a bit now with my nieces and nephews, but I'm still not comfortable with it.'

'I remember when I was about 12, my aunt and uncle came to visit with my cousin and her new baby,' said Normajeane, 34. 'They put the baby on my lap and I remember carefully sliding it slowly to the floor while they were talking. When they saw what I had done my aunt said: "Don't you want one someday?". My response was "I'd rather have a llama".'

You know that 'baby smell' that people talk about? It isn't pleasant to everyone. It must just be another of those things that we as non-parents will never understand nor want to understand.

Knowing your limits

Some women said they could not and do not want to 'have it all'. Perfectly capable people will now freely admit that having children would simply be too stressful and that they would be unable to cope.

'The whole superwoman thing is just too much,' said Helen, 33.

'I made my decision around the age of 21 after being around other people's children and thinking I wouldn't be able to cope,' said Maria, 23. Stress was something she mentioned throughout her responses.

'Some people would probably say I am selfish in not wanting to make room for a child in my life. I think I am realistic,' said Lyn, 44. 'I don't think that I would mentally cope very well with having a child around all the time. I would be stressed all the time and that in the long run is bad for my health.'

'I would continually worry about where they are or who they are with,' said Nicole, 23.

Admitting to a parent that you would not be able to cope is one of those things that gets bounced right back at you. 'Oh yes you would!', 'When you have them you find a way', 'You just *have* to cope'…but the truth is you *don't* have to. People have also suggested to us that knowing that you couldn't cope allows you to put coping mechanisms in place. So does that mean you should still have a child even if you know you can't cope? Give us a break!

Financial realities

Kids cost money. A lot of money. It is sometimes hard enough for a couple on average incomes to survive, let alone a single parent or low income family.

In an article in *The Sunday Telegraph* in April 1998, Bronwen Gora spoke to a family 'faced with staggering costs to raise their children'. The mother said she had to put the expense out of her mind. 'You become immune to it. It's expensive for everything,' she said. In the article, the Australian Family Association's Susan Bastick said shrinking family sizes had everything to do with the lack of job security, a decline in marriages and pressures on dual income families. 'The reality is it's too hard to be working and have too many kids. You can only split yourself so many ways,' Mrs Bastick said.

The article cited statistics from the Australian Institute of Family Studies, which said that in the five years to 1998, the annual cost of looking after a child aged between 11 and 13 rose by $1512 to $12 731 . In the same period the cost of bringing up a child aged between 8 and 10 has risen $1359 to $11 448 per year. These figures take into account expenses such as clothing, education and housing but, in reality, many parents spend far more than the average $36 to $39 per week when it comes to recreation and after-school activities.

More survey respondents listed finances as a benefit of being child-free rather than a reason to stay child-free. However, others simply felt that the financial pressures of a family would be too great, especially those people from low income families who have always struggled.

'Our family was always struggling for money,' said Marianne, 31. 'While I have a good job now I don't earn that much. I have enough trouble paying for those things that I need let alone having to pay for a child's expenses as well.'

Jane, 48, said that economic factors were very important to her and her then husband. 'My husband went to uni full time, then I did. It was a struggle to get a house and we had little money for travel. My first trip home [to the UK] in 1984 was to attend my father's funeral.'

'I have struggled in my younger years and do not wish to spend the rest of my life struggling, with no choices in life to do what I want to do,' said Kerry, 36.

Lack of financial resources leads more people to have children in their mid-thirties or not to have them at all. Anne, a 26-year-old public relations consultant, asked: 'What does this do to the population? Is it because economics tells us we have to work ten years longer than our parents did to be able to afford to bring up one child?'

Financial stability was Kerri's main reason for not having children. She is 26, has travelled widely and is now a driver for a brake company. 'I feel I have not yet obtained even a quarter of what I want. So how could I give a child what he or she needs let alone wants?' she said.

'I can't afford to [have kids],' said Karena, a 45-year-old artist and musician. 'I have been down the lower end of the socioeconomic ladder all my life. Having a child alters the amount of choice you have in life, and if it is already restricted by economic circumstances, it can completely change your career forever.'

'I'd have to quit some or all of my jobs,' said Julie, a TAFE teacher, massage therapist and rugby league strapper. 'I'm not used to relying on anyone else for income or asking for money. That would be too scary.'

Lack of financial security may be more important than lack of money in some cases. Busy small business owners are all too aware that their success depends on how hard they work, and how quickly it could all be taken away from them if the business fails.

'We have just invested much time and money in a small business operation and can't spare time or lost income to have a child,' said Kim, 29.

'We have our own business and I work full-time to feed us,' said Heather, 32. 'The business is struggling and I need to work. I feel that the first five years of a child's life is very important and I wouldn't like the idea of working full time and having someone else enjoy watching my child grow up.'

Would I make a 'good parent'?

While many parents take the child-free option as a criticism, it could be interpreted as a compliment because the child-free realise the enormity of the task. Many cheerfully admit to a lack of patience or inability to cope with the noise, mess or responsibility that children bring.

'I would much rather be classed as selfish than an unfit mother,' said Erica, who enjoys going out dining, drinking or dancing with her partner.

'I am not sure I have the patience or the temperament to devote myself to raising a child,' said Raquel, 27.

'I considered that my lack of "wanting" to be a parent may have made me a poor mother,' said Jan, 57. 'Crying babies send me troppo. I may have been a child basher.'

Susan J. & David L. Moore

'I would be a terrible mother,' said Helen, 33, the youngest of nine children. 'I have no patience or tolerance for children and cannot relate to them. I see too much of my own mother in myself, and although she wasn't a bad mother, she wasn't a particularly good mother either. I guess basically I don't like children. I have expressed to friends that one of my reasons for not having children is that I'm afraid I may become a child beater. I have no patience and when a complete stranger's child misbehaves, I want to hit it. I often get the response: "but it's different when it's your own". But how do you know? What if it isn't? It's a bit late then, isn't it. I don't believe it would be different. I think it would be just the same even if it is my own child. It would be a pretty risky experiment to find out that yes, I'm just as impatient and intolerant with my own child as I am with everyone else's.'

'As a career, parenting is too difficult,' said Julie, 37. 'Very few people do it well. I don't think I'd be good at it.'

Jacqui, 25, says she feels pressure to 'do it all' and that she would also have to be a perfect parent. 'The fact that there is no manual on raising the perfect, happy, well rounded child is frightening. The fear of failure, perhaps irreversible failure or error, is scary. How do you know if your methods are the best you can do?'

'I doubt my capacity for the tolerance and infinite selflessness I believe are required for the task,' said Theresa, 42.

'Our reasons are many, ranging from the environmental to the "selfish",' said Kirk, 28. 'In between, there is the nagging feeling that we would not be good and proper parents, who would have the time and offer it whenever it was demanded.' Kirk and his partner have full-time jobs and also work from home after hours teaching people to read.

'As the youngest in my family I didn't have to look after a baby at any time, as opposed to my two sisters who looked after me,' said Kathryn, 43. 'I therefore had no exposure to the care of a child and now feel totally inadequate if I have to hold one for more than a few minutes. I would not be a good parent.'

'I think I would have been one of those mothers to "push them out of the nest" ASAP,' said Kate, 55.

Aside from the individual's belief that they may not make a good parent, there are many groups out there telling us contradictory things about how to be a good parent. Some even say you shouldn't say 'no' to a child these days, unless you need to stop them running out onto the road. As a result the distinction between right and wrong, acceptable and unacceptable behaviour, becomes unclear to many parents. It is even less clear to the child. You now have to worry about how your neighbour may interpret your act of disciplining a child. Anything they hear over the fence could be reported to the authorities because 'you can't take any chances'. This all makes child-raising a very scary proposition, and more people worried that they may not be up to the task.

The parenthood trap

Many people are increasingly unwilling to trade lifestyle options for the trap of parenthood.

'Life is too exciting to be changing nappies and spending Saturdays at soccer!' said Sonia, 37.

There are so many career and recreational options available to child-free people, as discussed throughout this book. However, for many women, motherhood is simply not an attractive option. The reality is often very different from the perception.

Motherhood continues to be seen as woman's greatest achievement, yet...in practical terms, they are undervalued, unpaid, seen as unskilled and boring. Public and social facilities typically fail to cater for the needs of women with children. Recognising that child-rearing can be as monstrous as it is wonderful, women rightly feel ambivalent.

Jane Bartlett in Will you be mother? Women who choose to say no *(1997)*

Motherhood in itself is not an achievement. To 'achieve' is to finish. An 'achievement' is something accomplished. Motherhood is something that is never finished. It is with you until the day you die. But, aside from that, you don't actually have to do anything unusual to become a mother. Every member of the animal kingdom shows us that motherhood is a biological and instinct driven event. If every living thing on the planet can be a parent, then what is special about it? It is special to the person experiencing it, but that's about it.

Grant, 32, said one of the main reasons for choosing not to have a child is that the 'alleged benefits of parenthood are rarely realised. Many kids struggle with their parents from adolescence to adulthood. The supposed warm relationships are rarely realised,' he said.

'The majority of people I know with children are really struggling to hold their adult relationships together, time is so precious, and there are financial burdens,' said Tracey, 39. 'Having a child means that freedom would be lost, domesticity would be the order of the day, your sex life goes down the pan, you resort to cheap underwear (child-first, parent-last), your husband goes on the back burner, and before you know it your husband's having an affair because he can't hack the competition and you're a fish wife who can't afford to get her teeth cleaned at the dentist!'

The changing family

Despite the culture promoting motherhood in Australia, most women are very aware that mothers still get a raw deal. They are

43

increasingly unwilling to take on the carer's role alone, realising that, at the end of the day, they may not get the support they need from their partner and family.

Families are not so tightly knit and may be widely dispersed both geographically and socially or ideologically. Grandparents are often no longer willing to look after grandchildren other than the occasional turn at babysitting – most are active and busy in their own lives.

You're more likely to catch your mother sweating over a Jane Fonda aerobics video (hence the lack of ample lap) than a hot oven from which drifts the fragrant smell of a baking scone, and as for knitting useful garments in tiny sizes, forget it. Far too busy painting or sculpting. You'll be lucky if there's quality time for you, let alone your beloved offspring.

Felicity Biggins in The Australian, *30 January 1996*

'Being the female, it would turn my life upside down,' said Jill, 32. 'No working life for a while, less social contact, financial downturn and loss of a wage for a long period. I would feel less independent. From observation of my girlfriends, they almost go stir crazy, not having anyone to talk to for months, they are tired and run down. Two of my friends did it alone which was even tougher.'

Jane, 48, who moved to Australia from the UK said that she had 'no family support' and could not cope on her own. 'I have no family in Australia and can be isolated socially,' she said.

The only thing that would make Maria, 23, change her mind about having children would be her partner 'totally looking after the child, cleaning, cooking, teaching, etc'.

Anaïs, 38, has a very small family and in the past eleven years has lost her mother, aunt and both grandparents on her mother's side. 'The family support is just not there, which I consider quite important when thinking about having children,' she said.

'Neither one of us has any family support, for various reasons,' said Lori, 'and [having a child] would have restricted our lives greatly.'

Parents and child-free people agree that support from friends and family is essential. Certainly this is true of the people we know.

Parents jump at the chance of a small break and a night of romance. The traditional first option for support is the grandparents. The same people who may have had children to 'look after them in their old age' are now looking after their grandchildren 'in their old age'. Children are still being helped by their parents. So not only are they not being 'looked after' by their children, but their children are too busy to look after their own children. What makes us think that our generation will break this cycle?

Kids – their own worst enemy?

After creating heaven and earth, God created Adam and Eve. And the first thing He said to them was 'Don't.'

'Don't what?' Adam replied.

'Don't eat the forbidden fruit,' God said.

'Forbidden fruit? We got forbidden fruit? Hey, Eve, we got forbidden fruit!'

'No way!'

'Yes WAY!'

'Don't eat that fruit!' said God.

'Why?'

'Because I'm your Father and I said so!' said God, wondering why He hadn't stopped after making the elephants.

A few minutes later, God saw the kids having an apple break and was angry. 'Didn't I tell you not to eat that fruit?' the First Parent asked.

'Uh huh,' Adam replied.

'Then why did you?'

'I dunno,' Eve answered.

'She started it!' Adam said.

'Did not!'

'DID so!'

'DID NOT!'

Having had it with the two of them, God's punishment was that Adam and Eve should have children.

Anon.

We have often felt that being around kids for any great length of time can prove to be 'a natural contraceptive'. Having a child to stay for a week almost had us rushing to the clinic to be sterilised. Some of our survey respondents felt that spending time with the children of friends and relatives was enough to strengthen their decision not to have children, should they be having doubts.

'I don't hate them or even dislike them but when I see them my decision not to procreate is reinforced,' said Gabby, 32.

'I find children neither more interesting nor less annoying than their parents,' said Karena, 45. 'I don't automatically assume children will like me or respect me simply because I am an adult.'

'I don't mind babysitting every now and then, but seeing the intense change in lifestyle that children bring, and the parents' inability to do what they would really like to do, only re-affirms my belief that children are not for me,' said Nicole, 23.

'Some children are interesting and amusing, some aren't – just as it is with adults,' said Trudi, who chose a career over marriage and children in the late 1970s when she believed these were the only two options. 'I could be heard grinding my teeth the day that one mother told her daughter and playmates "that woman doesn't like children" in a tone that suggested I was some evil witch who might cook them for dinner.'

'I want to strangle them at times,' said Fiona, 32. 'As I have very little contact with children, I have very little patience with them. Well, close to none actually. Yes, I am the person saying "I was never allowed to do that as a kid." Any judgement I make tends to be negative. I guess I just don't see "cute".'

Maria, 23, also says she has become 'very judgmental' about children and keeps thinking, 'I wouldn't let them get away with that!'

'I really am quite intolerant of naughty, cheeky children but feel drawn towards some others who are well behaved and interesting,' said Lorraine, 52. 'Also, I just love cuddling very tiny babies. Oddly children often seem to really like me.'

'I don't enjoy it when they dominate an adult party or meeting by doing a "circus" act,' said Stephanie, 41.

Leanne, a police officer, says the way the world is today means that parents have no control. 'They try try try to do the best they know how – I don't want to feel like that,' she said. 'I don't think I would like to be faced with today's issues as a child, teen or young adult, so I am not about to "drop a child" in it.'

'I have been a good actress in the past, holding babies and playing with toddlers but these days I just can't be bothered,' said Normajeane, 34. 'The older I get the less I'm pandering to pressures put on us by parents to find their children adorable. It's great that they think their kids are the most beautiful, smart, funny kids in the world but I don't like being put in a position where I have to agree with them. And from now on, any friend that makes me talk to their toddler on the phone is no longer a friend. Most children under the age of 8 are dead boring 99% of the time and when I visit their parents I don't want to spend my time pretending to enjoy their conversation about Thomas the Tank Engine.'

'My job uses up all my energy and goodwill,' said Anne, a high school teacher. 'I'd pity a child of mine left with my mood at the end of a long day...'

Anne may see another side of education more vividly than the rest of us. There is evidence of a breakdown in respect for authority in the system. As children we were fearful of doing anything wrong. We would never have thought of walking out of a class, or assaulting a teacher verbally or physically. Legislation and different community standards have brought about a situation where there are few serious consequences for a lot of student behaviour. Teachers like Anne probably see a youth that they would not want their own child spending time with.

I forgot to have kids!

Some people simply delay having children for years, until one day they realise they are happy without them – not having made a conscious decision about it.

'The decision became more permanent as I got older,' said Tracie, 35. 'I always felt "non-maternal", but used to believe this would change – it hasn't. At the end of my marriage around 1992 I finally admitted to myself that I wasn't suited to or interested in having children.'

'In my mid-twenties I thought I'd better set an age to have kids, seeing as all my friends had,' said Louise, 32. 'So I said when I was 30 I would have kids. Well when 30 came around I realised I wasn't anywhere near ready to be a parent – this was soon followed by not wanting to be a parent ever.'

'I've just never met the right person to have kids with,' said Tracey, 39. 'I always thought I wanted kids, but I'm doing so much now that I'll be perfectly happy if I don't. Time is running out but I'm not concerned at all.'

Child-free relationships

A number of research reports have found that child-free marriages last longer and are happier than those with children. For all the joys of parenthood, the arrival of a baby marks a long drop in marital happiness that is at its lowest during a child's teenage years, according to a US survey of 6785 spouses by sociologist Mary Benin of Arizona State University, Tempe, quoted in an article in USA Today on 12 August 1997. Other studies have found a similar U-shaped curve for couple contentment.

When a baby arrives there is an abrupt transition from an adult to a baby centred household. As children grow, households get more hectic, and teenage outbursts can upset marriages further. Happiness takes an upturn when kids at home are over the age of 18, but then husbands feel more happily married than wives, according to Benin. The report found that childless couples are as happy as couples before babies arrive. Without the buffeting cycles of child-rearing, they tend to stabilise at this high level over time, Benin said.

Modern partnerships are more egalitarian than those even a few decades ago, when most husbands expected their wives to have children. Now most young Australian men prefer an 'equal' partner with a good income.

The bargaining power of today's women is largely a result of their contribution to the family income, and means that decisions about marriage, home and family are now mostly made jointly.

Maintaining an equal relationship

An Australian National University survey published in October 1998 found that women are reluctant to have children because they want to maintain an 'equal' relationship with their partners and do not want to lose the bargaining power of paid work.

The study, based on a national survey of 2231 couples, found 10% had decided not to have children. The report's author, Edith Gray, said that people who do not want children in the future have a more equitable relationship and have negotiated a situation where they can both pursue their life interests.

Childless couples were twice as likely to share household chores equally. But once women became mothers, they were twice as likely to do all the cleaning, shopping, ironing, washing and cooking. While young women are educated to higher levels than men in corresponding age groups, according to the ANU survey, the responsibility for child-rearing and household work still lies with the woman.

Enjoying each other's company

Many of our survey respondents expressed a reluctance to 'spoil' the happy and equal relationship they enjoy with their partner.

'Our relationship is not a "pedestrian" one, we are king and queen in our own respective castles, we have careers and feel fulfilled and content with our lot,' wrote Julia, 38. 'We are considering writing a book one day about our choice of lifestyle, to raise people's awareness that the "pedestrian" lifestyle followed by most is not necessarily right for most.'

'We have both been married prior to this, to partners who did want children, and this proved to be a problem and ultimately contributed to the marriage breakdown,' said Kathryn, 43.

'Apart from this, for the last ten years we have enjoyed an intensely close relationship, which we treasure and would hate to jeopardise by having to share ourselves with another person. We have often seen how this can change a partnership when one person feels neglected.'

CHILD-FREE ZONE

'We have a wonderful, adult lifestyle – which means we can be who we are, not role play "mother", "wife", "family unit",' said Karena, 45. 'We are free to explore our lives and live fully.'

'Many women with children say they wish they had made a similar decision,' said Ros, 45. 'Some have said they think my relationship with my partner has endured so long (25 years) because we didn't have kids. Many of my girlfriends are single parents.'

On the subject of child-free partnerships, Sonia, 37 feels that 'you can sometimes become too self-absorbed.'

With or without children, a relationship needs to have some kind of outcome, whether it is the achievement of common goals or a growth in understanding and trust. Child-free relationships need to evolve or risk becoming stale. The most wonderful thing is the time that you will have for each other, and the freedom you'll have to pursue other goals, both together and separately.

'We have watched many of our friends' marriages end in divorce,' said Jan, 57. 'Others have had numerous hassles with their children which have caused problems in their relationships with their partners. I do accept that they may have had a great deal of pleasure and love from their kids – sometimes.'

There is so much right about our child-free relationship that it just cannot be the wrong decision for us. The flexibility we have as individuals, and quite different individuals in many ways, would be severely compromised by having a single all-consuming focus thrust upon us. We do different things. Our different interests enhance each other's lives. The different goals we have and the different paths that we take do not compromise our partnership.

Susan J. & David L. Moore

As a man (not only a woman's choice)

Anthropologists tell us that men are designed to be promiscuous. Men are supposed to have sex with as many females as possible to ensure that our species carries on the best and healthiest genes. This sits pretty well with the average male who, at this point in time, will be overcome with an intense desire to elbow his partner, saying 'See, I told you honey.' The female of the species is supposed to trap the male and give him good reasons for hanging around to look after her.

A recent TV documentary demonstrated that human spermatozoa come in three distinctive types. There are the swimmers, the decoys and the attackers. The swimmer's job is to go like hell for the egg. The attacker's job is to hunt and kill foreign sperm. The decoy's job was to attract foreign hunter sperm. The documentary had graphic and amusing footage of this taking place. The obvious question for our modern monogamous world is 'why?' Well, the 'shag anything that moves' theory means that inevitably there is going to be some 'mixing'. So, it seems that science (probably via male scientists) is telling us that it's quite okay to roam. It results in the survival of the fittest.

As you grow up it seems that some things are inevitable. Aside from death and taxes, when you get married you have children. Of course, most of us do want to have sex. You can take all the precautions available to a male and even discuss the 'what ifs' of pregnancy with partners. If you don't want kids, aside from making you look caring, it allows you to judge how fast you have to get out of the relationship. Suddenly you have a real empathy with the cave guy, and you didn't even know you had killer sperm. However, where we thought the cave guy was running to have sex, and a baby, with every cave chick, suppose that he was actually running because he *knew* what babies were and didn't feel like hanging around.

'My wife wanted children – not now but in the near future. We have separated now because of this (and a lot of other reasons). But on this matter I felt it was selfish of me to deprive her of kids,' said Chris, 28.

'I did not want children and felt frightened of being trapped into it,' said Stewart, 35. 'It makes finding a partner more difficult. But luckily working in law has meant I've met a number of women who were unwilling to give up what they had worked so hard for and I can't see them ever being mothers. I still haven't met the "right person", but certainly haven't given up hope that I will one day. In the meantime I just get on with it.'

When you meet a partner who also does not want to have children, all the 'difficulties' of the monogamous long-term relationship seem to disappear. Suddenly you don't want to run away. We had a particularly short engagement and knew quickly that we were not going to let each other get away. Marriage no longer equated to children. Hence the commitment that it entailed was embraced by both of us. We know that we're not going to have children. As a result we don't have to, nor do we want to, run away. We are lucky – it's not so easy when expectations differ.

Susan J. & David L. Moore

The benefits of being child-free

Financial freedom

Raising a child costs a lot of money. If you don't have children, then that money can be used elsewhere. Pretty simple really. But this point alone is probably the biggest reason why child-free people are called selfish. It seems as though we have more money, and the trappings of having more money, when the reality is that we have the same money, but we spend it differently. If you want to spend it on a child, that is your choice. If you want to spend it on a holiday, that is simply another choice. It could be argued that each provides a degree of pleasure.

We have already mentioned the annual cost of having a child. It is not an insignificant amount and obviously your lifestyle can be seriously impacted by this amount unless you are wealthy.

Up until our recent purchase of a house, we did not owe anybody a cent. No credit cards being paid off, no car loans or leases, no hire purchase payments or personal loans. What is ours is ours. We suspect that not many parents can claim the same.

Now that we have the mortgage, we are in a position to pay it off quickly. However, we still have a desire to enjoy life. So, without any need to build an empire to pass on, we don't actually have to pay it off quickly. There are other reasons why we want to, but one of the reasons isn't to accommodate our children if we die prematurely.

An adaptable lifestyle

Young people are now used to change and choice – in fact, the current work environment requires people to remain flexible and open to change. They make decisions every day about their education, career, travel, lifestyle and residence that their parents would not have had to make at such a young age. Is it any surprise then that more and more young people are choosing to delay or avoid the inflexible and permanent role of parenthood?

'Hopefully, whatever future I have, childless or otherwise, it will be a future that I deliberately engineered, a future of choice,' said Raquel, 27.

Roger and his wife Jacki moved to Australia after being married for less than a year. 'I'm not sure where we may go next,' said Roger, 'but being child-free allows us the most freedom in jobs, places to live and even countries to live in.'

To Christine, a 39-year-old hotel manager, the main benefit is that 'we are able to do as we please, from "what will we have for dinner" to "let's move house – now".'

Kerri, 26, said freedom was the main benefit of being of child-free. 'Our lifestyle just wouldn't allow for the time it takes to organise kids. We can hardly organise ourselves let alone someone else,' she said.

> 'Freedom is my choice,' said Tracey, 39. 'That's why we don't have a mortgage either – we can take flight whenever. I've got a million things I want to do for the rest of my life, and washing sick-bibs is definitely not one of them!'

William, 53, says the only benefit of being child-free is 'lack of pressure'. He said he did not want to be 'an activities organiser for ten years and an ogre for the next eight'.

'I don't have a permanent emotional and practical "stone around my neck",' said Kate, 55. 'Mothers are never completely free of their children.'

At a recent dinner party a friend and his very pregnant wife were asking people about their opinions on schools. Apparently, if you want to get your child into a good private school you have to book before it is born and then pay a yearly fee to keep the position until your child attends the school. This included high school, some twelve years after the child's birth. How ridiculous – it is one thing to plan your future, it is another thing to tie it down. How many people know what they'll be doing in twelve years?

Career flexibility

'Not having children has given me the freedom to do as much or as little as I like in my life,' said Karena, a 45-year-old artist and musician. 'I would never want to resent my children for making it necessary for me to sacrifice my own interests. Children should be hugely desired and cherished. This means that my career is my own fault – successful or not I can't blame anyone else for it. You are totally responsible for your own life if you elect not to have children.'

'The effect on our careers has only been positive,' said Christine, manager of a tourist facility. 'We have been able to pick and choose career changes without having to worry about kids, friends of kids and schools.'

Stephanie, a 41-year-old sales executive in the information technology industry, says she is 'taken seriously as a woman in a competitive environment'. As she is child-free, she can afford the time and energy to compete on the same terms as men.

Lorraine, 52, feels that staying child-free has allowed her 'the luxury of doing just what I love doing. If I had had children, I would not have felt comfortable … continuing my career as a long-haul flight attendant,' she said.

CHILD-FREE ZONE

Brian and his wife emigrated from New Zealand 'to improve our job prospects. I believe we would have hesitated, and possibly lost the opportunities, had we had children,' he said.

Lyn, 44, stopped working for a time in 1992 and says that being child-free meant she could change jobs when she pleased. 'At one stage I resigned because I hated my job, I was single and went without work for three months, without the dole. I couldn't have done that with a family. I was also able to work shifts without having to worry about anybody else and attend interstate meetings as they arose.'

'While interviewing for my current position, my employer was dancing around the question he knew to be illegal so I answered it without his asking: 'No I cannot and will not be having children",' said Betty, a 47-year-old accountant. 'I have worked for him for ten years now and I have wonderful freedom (I telecommute) and respect in my job.'

'My career is my passion and I feel that my success is due to the time and energy I have to devote to it,' said Janelle, a 33-year-old self-employed importer.

Laura, a 41-year-old doctor, says that not having children had had 'a huge effect' on her career. 'I was initially a clinical psychologist then decided to study medicine at age 30, completing my degree at 36, then undertaking my resident medical officer years. That would not have been possible for me if I'd had a child. Some people "achieve" it, but I've never wanted to try to "have it all" as I see that as a trap. Life's hard enough as it is!'

'As I have not been particularly ambitious or in the corporate world, I'm not sure that having kids would have made a lot of difference,' said Lyndall, 47. 'But I have been an obsessive student. That would have been harder to achieve.'

Julie is a TAFE teacher, a massage therapist and a strapper for rugby league players and says she certainly couldn't do these three jobs if she had a child. 'Imagine a baby stroller in the football sheds!' she said. 'I have had an interesting and varied career, based around a large flexibility factor. I can change course at will and not worry much about income or working hours. No wonder my sister says she hates me – she's joking – I think!'

Genevieve, 39, says that remaining child-free has had an 'enormous, huge, tremendous' effect on her career. 'I completed an undergraduate degree in science, with an honours year, and much later a Masters of Business Administration, with distinction. I have been a factory manager, an operations manager, a general manager of operations in Canada, and a state manager with a large public company. The company operates in a very male dominated area, and I set many records for being the first woman in numerous positions. I believe that if I had [had] children I would not have achieved the levels, the results or the career structure that I have. I now have my own business as a professional speaker. I am very independent and work very hard. Again I don't believe I could have achieved the success I have if I had children and especially if I was the primary child carer.'

'I have always found it very easy to get work, particularly shift work,' said Gabby, 32. 'I think it may have something to do with my availability at all times. Otherwise I don't believe [being child-free] has had much of an effect. There are a lot of successful working mums out there too.'

Stephanie, 36, enjoys her career as a psychologist. 'I have time and energy to perform my duties properly,' she said. 'I do not go home from a stressful day having to meet the needs of others.'

Tracey, 39, an ex-hairdresser who is studying to be an astrologer, also says the effect on her career has been very positive. 'I mean, who wants an employee who has heaps of time off when the kid gets sick?' she said.

'Remaining child-free has had a significant impact on our careers,' said Normajeane, 34. 'Financially, we would never have been able to start our own business and I wouldn't have had the time to pursue a career as an artist.'

Raquel, a landscape architect, also recently left a highly paid, salaried job to start her own business. 'Perhaps this was foolish,' she said, 'but at present my decision affects no one but myself. I am able to make decisions based on what I want from life, not on what I need to do to maintain a child.'

'Obviously the fact that I can continue to work without taking time off for children is a big plus from an employer's point of view, though I am not hugely career minded,' said Helen, 33. 'The company I work for is very "family values" oriented and coming back to work after having a baby is not encouraged. Management believes that a mother's place is at home with the baby.'

'I've always enjoyed being available at that particular moment when there were heights in my career,' said Sally, 51. 'I also feel that being childless helped me get jobs on a number of occasions. Even though employers aren't allowed to ask you whether you have children, you may volunteer the information that you don't have any.'

'I have been able to change occupations and try all sorts of jobs,' said Kathryn, 43, a secretary. 'I have been able to work full time, whatever hours and not catch colds from children. It seems any bug that's going around at school is brought home. My colleagues with children often fall sick through their kids' sickness.'

A colleague has just had his third child. Each time he suggests that a child is old enough to be left in day care and that his wife may want to get a job, or an interest at least, another child comes along. His career flexibility is being narrowed. By his own admission he'll have to strive for higher paying jobs or work longer hours to cater for the increasing financial burden.

Healthy living

'I see very few negatives to being child-free,' said Sarah, 37. 'My health does not suffer because of sleepless nights; I don't have back pain or piles caused by pregnancy or childbirth. I don't have tummy muscles that have lost their elasticity because of having a Caesarean section. I believe I have less stress than people with children as I don't have to worry about their well being, health, education and so on.'

An RMIT University study, reported in the Sun Herald on 13 December 1998, found that post-natal depression, a common concern of women, is also suffered by 1 in 16 men. Six per cent of men developed depression after becoming fathers. The article also cited a survey from the Institute of Psychiatry in London which echoed the finding, with 7% of fathers in the Bristol area becoming depressed, teary, irritable and unable to cope after the birth of a child.

'I didn't want the physical, mental and emotional involvement with another being,' said Sally, 51. 'I felt it was too hard to be a parent. There are so many pressures and duties and there are problems like drugs, unemployment and youth suicide. [The main benefit to being child-free is] life is so worry-free.'

Stress is a modern day plague and it is being attributed to many modern ills. It can't be denied that children do cause great amounts of stress and for some people that is simply too much.

More time for your partner

'Grant and I are best friends, we do everything and go everywhere together,' said Normajeane, 34. 'I think you lose part of that when you become a family, there are a lot of problems that can come between you. A friend of mine who recently started a family told me that your relationship is never the same again after the kids come along.'

'I am able to put all my energies into my partner and concentrate on making a marriage work,' said Tracey, 39. 'We have loads of time for each other. The benefit is, we are really happy and we love and adore each other – I don't need any more than that.'

'You can stay with your partner because you want to, not because you have to,' said Sally, 51.

'Personal time between my wife and I is very very special,' said John, 37. 'I guess this special time would be limited if children were present. I would find it difficult to balance these feelings.'

'We look forward to our relationship continuing to grow stronger year by year, as it has these first eleven years,' said Betty, 47. 'We are unhampered by the trials of children's dramas. Unlike many of our married-with-children friends, we actually know each other very well and love to have time alone together. So many of our breeding friends are either unable or unwilling to even escape alone together for a single weekend. Perhaps with the priorities of family life, they no longer know each other well enough to be comfortable in only each other's company? I see us maintaining a high quality of life together with satisfying professional lives and romantic holidays, unencumbered by family demands.'

'Not having a child means that I can give my partner and myself more,' said Leanne, 34. 'I live for us and what we want to achieve to be happy. I am content with my choice of partner and I don't feel I have to supplement our relationship with a "product". I can have sex when I want it and my money is spent on us.'

Youth and vitality

'Another consideration (and I am not normally vain) is that at 43, I look 35 as I have kept my figure. My body hasn't suffered from the pushing and pulling of skin! Or varicose veins,' writes Kathryn, a secretary.

Anaïs, 38, listed 'being able to continue an active sex life' as one of the main benefits of being child-free. Many women report a loss of interest in sex after childbirth, which can last up to two years after the baby is born. Some of our friends can attest to this.

Fiona, 32, saw the main benefit of staying child-free as 'being able to keep thinking young'.

John, 42, sees the main benefit as 'retaining my personal identity as "John the person" rather than being so-and-so's father, and being able to maintain a "younger" outlook in life.'

'Another big benefit to being child-free is that you don't have to grow up,' said Normajeane, 34. 'We are a lot "younger" than our parent friends and a lot more involved in leisure activities. Basically, I would say that we have more fun.'

No regrets

'If I had my time again...'

Few people with children truly regret having them, and cite the joy of seeing their offspring develop into an adult as the main benefit. However, some feel that they did not have a choice and, given the opportunity to live their lives over again, they would not have children next time around.

'One friend, who is a parent of some great kids, always tells me how sensible my decision is, and if I ever have any doubts I'm sure she will remind me,' said Louise, 32.

Normajeane, 34, knows several people who have told her they wish they had made the same decision and felt pressured into having a family. 'The people who call us selfish are usually people who are dissatisfied with their family life and jealous of the freedom that we still have,' she said. 'Unfortunately, the decision to have a child is not a reversible one and once people realise that real motherhood is not as magical as it is in books, films and television, it's usually too late.'

Karena, 45, lives in a small community where child-free couples are rare. 'My friends fall into two camps – the envious (who have children) and the waverers (who can see how happy I am, but the hormones are insisting). Some friends who have children tell me how smart I am and not to change.'

'My brother, who has a son (the son is now in his twenties) has said if he had his time over again he would choose not to have children,' said Tony, 45.

Family and friends of Leanne, 34, have said to her 'Don't do what I did and get talked into it', 'I thought it would help my marriage', 'Good on you – it's not what it's made out to be', 'You're lucky to have a partner [who] agrees' and 'I wish I knew what I was getting into, you're lucky to know how you feel'.

On the other hand, none of our older survey respondents regretted their decision to stay child-free. Some are very aware that they have 'missed' something, but do not feel that their lives would have been better if they'd had children.

'I chose not to have children as early as 1957, and have never regretted it,' said Margaret, 66. 'The reasons I gave were that we married to spend time with one another rather than bringing up children – children had nothing to do with our decision to marry. The second reason was that even as early as that, many people saw the future of the world as bleak environmentally. *Silent Spring* by Rachel Carson had a great impact on our generation. It appeared likely that the world would not be a fit place for future generations to inherit. The nuclear threat was very real then and while some people don't see bombs as a threat anymore, the problem of nuclear waste is still with us.

'Because we had no children of our own we had time to enrich the lives of other children, some of my sisters', some of my friends'. We had the time and resources to introduce them to aspects of life their parents could not provide, or anyway, did not. Books, music, plays, nature: in fact, the richness that can become an unattainable luxury in a busy family.'

Margaret worked as a high school teacher and spent many years away from Australia, including a period as a tour guide in York, England, a job that gave her much pleasure. At the age of 24 she married Don, then 40 years old. She says that as articulate, politically aware people they moved mostly among educated people who respected their choice. Margaret said she knew an English couple who later regretted not having children.

Vivienne, 59, said she has not felt a moment of regret. 'I don't feel child deprived,' she said. 'I have eleven nephews and nieces whom I adore and am in continuous contact with. They love to have a single aunt who is like a friend to them. Some friends' children call me "the cool auntie".

'I have many artistic and literary interests for which you need loads of free, uninterrupted time on a constant basis. This is impossible if you have children. I am in my middle years now, but I made the child-free choice in my teens. I didn't like what I saw around me as far as the role of women was concerned. They didn't seem to have much of a life apart from the domestic scene and there was little creativity, spontaneity and humour in their lives.

'I don't think about these matters in as black and white a manner as I did when I was younger, since I believe that marriage and children can be a great, convenient, life-enriching arrangement. However, because of the way society functions in most Western cultures, the experience of having children often brings with it all kinds of social, economic and even spiritual burdens, which make life rather joyless for people.'

Ultimately, whether we have children or not, our lives can be rich and wonderful. None of the child-free people we have spoken to have ever regretted their decision and feel in many ways that they are at a distinct advantage to those who have children. However, as with people who have children, we feel that few people are prepared to admit that they regret a choice they have made.

Susan J. & David L. Moore

What is the cost of being child-free?

Friends who become parents

When people become parents it is natural that their time pressures and priorities change. It is also normal that when they do socialise, many prefer to spend time with other parents. The unfortunate side effect is that child-free people can suddenly find their circle of friends dwindling. Losing friends who are parents means child-free people often have to make a special effort to make new social contacts.

Suzanne, 32, suddenly felt very isolated this year when she realised that in her circle of close friends, she was the only one without children. 'I resent the fact that when I visit them, I deliberately don't talk about my work and what I did on the weekend. They just aren't interested and give me the impression that what I do is not important or worthwhile. I want to tell everyone about the conference I went to in the US or that we're going to visit family in Scotland for our next holiday, but instead I listen to them talk about their kids for hours on end. I feel both bored and shut out.'

'I guess it's just a social thing of being a little bit different, a little bit "suss",' said Pauline, 55. 'Most people find it a bit suss, especially if you get stroppy about it and make the point that you are very happy. I'm very happy with things the way they are. I've also had to walk away from a lot of conversations that I can't be bothered listening to because it's all about other people's kids.'

'At times I also feel like [my wife and I are] social outcast[s],' said John, 42, 'as most of our friends have children and they all want to do children's things, and we are on the bottom of their priority list.'

'It's difficult to keep friends when they start a family because they get obsessed with baby and all that goes with baby,' said Tracey, 39. 'They tend to mix with people with kids. I don't like having people visiting me who've got kids, they mess up my house and I'm not used to the mess and noise. I feel like I'm being fussy and anti-social, but the parents should also respect my property. I've lost many friends.

'Friends expect me to adore their children, as they do. I try and put on a good face and pretend to be interested. Frankly they bug me, especially if they're under five years old, out of control, wreckers of homes, pushing crusts of bread into videos and the like – it makes my skin crawl.

'A while ago an old friend called me up and told me she was pregnant with her second child. I said to her, "you poor thing!" In hindsight, I could have been more tactful, but I just blurted out my first gut reaction. Oh well, that's life.'

'I have a friend of fifteen years who has two boys,' said Tracie, 35. 'I am their godmother, however I make very little effort to see them, which is awful I know, but the times we do see them the occasion revolves around the kids.'

'I find it hard to find like-minded women who can hold a conversation on anything other than what their child is doing at present. Hopefully in another ten years or so I will be mixing with women whose children will have left home (and may be wondering what to do with their lives) and I may be more accepted,' wrote Kathryn, 43.

'Our old friends who have children often don't invite us to parties or functions because they think we wouldn't enjoy it with children around,' said John, 37.

'I would like to talk to people in the same situation as myself but [everyone I know has] children. I do not have friends and do not know anyone in the same situation as myself,' wrote Edith, 36. She also expressed an interest in forming a support group.

Organisations for child-free people exist in the US and the UK, but not in Australia yet. In the US, the Child-Free Association provides support and information to those who have chosen not to have children and those who are undecided and want more information. It publishes a newsletter and a booklet called 'Living Child-Free'. The group's Internet web site (www.child-free.com) also offers a bulletin board and links to other articles and resources for child-free people. There is a group called 'No Kidding! ' (www.nokidding.bc.ca) which also has chapters in the US and Canada. The British Organisation of Non-Parents was a similar group mentioned in a number of our references, but we could not confirm that it is still operating. Internet discussion groups also exist that cater for child-free people all over the world. At times these forums can seem like one long 'whinge' about parents and children. But when you think that child-free people are normally unable to voice their opinions on these topics because it is not socially acceptable to do so, these forums definitely have a place.

'Recently I have become more selfish about letting friends just disappear from my life when they have kids,' said Dave, 32. 'I am in the middle of an experiment right now where I am setting the expectations for a friend who is pregnant. The first thing I told her, when I found out that she was pregnant, was that I wasn't going to babysit and that I still expected to socialise with her. I asked her what her plans were for maintaining a social life and who was going to babysit while we went out? She has understood my position on children for some time, and even though she finds it amusing and can't quite work out whether I am serious or not, she knows that she doesn't have to hide from me when the baby is born. She also knows that I am happy that she is happy.'

Where is my tax going?

The child-free are the most taxed but the least benefited group in Australia today. In an *Australian Financial Review* economic briefing in June 1996, Dr David Clark of the University of NSW School of Economics analysed household income and expenditure data to determine the effects of taxes and benefits on different households in Australia.

CHILD-FREE ZONE

Dr Clark found that the group hit the hardest is households of one couple with no children. In 1996, they received on average $66 per week in benefits from government spending but paid $276 in taxes. The value of benefits is low compared with other groups because they do not receive income support, family payments, education benefits, or rent assistance. They make less use of government funded health services than either aged households or households with children. On the other hand, their relative tax burden is high because such households have higher average incomes – although not all are Dinks (dual income, no kids).

The whole idea of tax is to contribute towards the cost of government and provide money for essential infrastructure and services for the benefit of all. However, many child-free people resent the fact that they are forever paying for services they will never need and, at worst, for other people's lack of forethought and planning (especially family planning). Some also believe they should be compensated for their lack of reliance on government funds.

'I believe strongly that it is me who should be receiving incentives from the government not to have children,' said Kate, 55, a fine art restorer and active environmentalist. 'I have to support the community's irresponsibility.'

'My husband feels that child-free couples are discriminated against in regard to so much of our taxes subsidising the health care and education of others' children, but that bothers me little,' said Laura, a 41-year-old doctor.

Susan J. & David L. Moore

'Who cares if the tax system or social welfare discriminates in favour of families?' said Karena, 45. 'They deserve all the help they can get.'

'Certainly the tax structure is set up to [benefit] the breeding part of the public, to financially advantage them because they have chosen to have children,' said Betty, 47. 'Some people feel because they have children everyone else should support their decision through government funded childcare and other subsidies. Yes, there is an obligation to which we happily contribute to provide education and medical care for all members of society, but it is inequitable to ask one part of the community to financially underwrite the baby-making decisions of the other half, particularly when the "need" for a second parent to work is sometimes only to afford a second car or a VCR.'

'I think there is a political bias towards families which leaves singles somewhat worse off. For instance, my boyfriend is unemployed and when he went to get a pair of prescription glasses, asked if there were any concessions available. He was told only people with children were eligible. That sucks,' said Marianne, 31.

When politicians in election campaigns address women voters, the debate centres on childcare places, school funding and family benefits. Politicians have not yet realised that almost a quarter of women today will not have a family of their own. Singles and childless couples represent a large group of people whose needs are not addressed by 'family policy'. While politicians may promote a return to 'family values', their policies are not enough to encourage more women to have families.

'I believe there is a lot of emphasis put on families, childcare, family allowances and so on,' said Tracie, 35. 'I resent paying my taxes to pay for other people's children.'

CHILD-FREE ZONE

When you're in the economic commentary business, you soon learn that it's not hard to make yourself unpopular. Something I learnt early on, for instance, is that it's not wise to echo the commonly held view among economists that the decision to have kids is an act of consumption.

With the advent of effective contraception, this is a point of view that's grown in persuasiveness and pertinence. These days, almost all couples exercise their freedom to decide how many children to have, and a growing minority decide not to have any.

If I decide to have a family, whereas you decide to buy a boat or take more overseas holidays, why does that make me more virtuous and deserving than you?

Surely, we've merely decided to gratify ourselves – and spend our incomes – in differing ways.

What's more, your decision to avoid having kids has saved the taxpayer a bundle in childcare, education, health-care and other costs.

Ross Gittins in the Sydney Morning Herald, *15 September 1999*

According to Normajeane, 34, the negative to being child-free is that 'we don't exist' in the government's eyes. She feels very strongly that child-free couples are discriminated against by government and non-government organisations, and provides a number of examples:

'The government seems to be of the opinion that all married couples either have children, will have children or are attending fertility clinics to find out why they can't. According to a couple we know who were on the IVF program, the government pays them back a large proportion of the cost and yet we had no help in paying for Grant's vasectomy. And several years ago, Grant was working in the family business for less than the basic wage. I was picking up some work here and there but things were very tight. At the time, we had a couple of friends considered by the government to be low income families. They had free health care, lots of government subsidies and quite a healthy cash handout. Both of these families had nice houses and spent a lot of money on entertainment, junk food and holidays. One of them put in an in-ground swimming pool and the other a spa. We were living in a half-built house and didn't know if we would be able to pay the bills. I wrote several letters to the paper and different political parties hoping that someone could explain to me why we didn't exist, but to no avail.

'A friend of ours who runs a garage carried out a large repair job on a car belonging to a single mother. She decided not to pay the bill and he took her to court with no success. Lawyers told him that no court will prosecute a single mother and to kiss his money goodbye. Since then I have heard similar stories from other tradesmen. Why do we pay and mothers go free?'

Single income and multiple child families just seem to want more for less, just because 'kids are the future'. Are they, if we can't afford to do the best for them?

Some years ago a family with six children and a seventh on the way appeared on an evening current affairs TV show complaining that they couldn't afford to have their children wear school uniforms or go on school excursions. Public education was getting too expensive. When the reporter dared to ask why they kept on having children, when they were obviously struggling to feed and clothe the ones they had, the mother replied, 'We just love children, and children are the future.' What kind of future will those kids have? Surely if you really love children, you want to be able to give them the best possible start in life, and if you can only afford to do this for one or two children, then so be it.

'And what about the mother of two who patronised me for not wanting children only two nights ago, [and] who actually confessed to occasions where she had to decide whether to feed her children or buy cigarettes?' said Kirk, 28.

'From a tax perspective, having a family certainly has more advantages,' said Anaïs, 38.

Child-free people are often reminded of the aging population and that having less children means fewer people to work to support us in our old age. The arguments don't hold much water, because a social security system is by nature artificial and should be adjusted to reflect changes in populations. Child-free people are also often less likely to need support in their old age.

The family may not understand

Pressure from family, including parents, in-laws, siblings and even partners can be subtle or quite intense.

'My ex-husband wanted children,' said Stephanie, 41. 'There was enormous pressure from him and his family and friends.' She says that they 'harassed and belittled' her constantly. 'However, my family totally accepted and supported my choice,' she said.

'My mother was horrified when I told her at 21 I didn't want children,' said Betty, now 47. 'She told me I was giving up woman's greatest joy. Her generation had limited opportunities to consider alternatives so I guess she had to think her mothering was a major achievement or think her life had been wasted.'

'My husband's family is large, European and Catholic – a bad combination for a couple who want to remain child-free,' said Sarah, 37. 'While no overt pressure has been brought to bear, subtle factors are at work.' She recalled an incident that occurred not long after her marriage. 'I had been working long hours for many weeks and had one Saturday afternoon off so I went to bed for a short nap. One of my husband's aunts called in and, when told that I was napping, asked if I was resting because I was pregnant!'

'Only one of my brothers has children and he keeps saying: "You've got nothing in your life – you've got no kids",' said Tracey, 39. 'A lot of my other friends and relatives think this also, and I feel, generally, society thinks this too. Not that I care!'

'Mum and Dad were pretty disappointed with me at first, but got over it when my siblings "came good",' wrote Julie, 37. 'Mum was worried about what other people would think. My mother-in-law thought I was smart. My sister loves me I'm sure but is a little envious of my lifestyle – she has said so.'

As the older of two daughters, Christine, 39, is also glad that 'the pressure is off' since her sister had two children. Although she made her decision clear to her family, they did not believe or accept it. 'I recently had to spend the day in hospital for gyno surgery under general anaesthetic,' she said. 'The doctors and nurses were all amazed that it was my first stay in a hospital since I was born in one. They all said: 'Did you have your children at home, then?' Astonishment was the general reaction when I loudly stated that I had no children, by choice. 'After the surgery I rang my father to tell him I was fine, and he said, "So now will you be able to conceive?". I was speechless and angry and disappointed that he hadn't bothered to listen to a word I'd said over the last 20 years.'

George, 25, said that at the beginning of his relationship with his partner, when they discovered that neither of them wanted children, they told their parents and friends and were laughed at and told they'd change their minds. When that didn't work we were told we had a moral obligation to have children, he said. 'They try and take the moral stand - "if we'd made the same decision you wouldn't be here today" - which is fair enough, but a lot has changed in 25 years.'

'We have not really discussed our decision with family or friends, although I think they realise. They tend to treat our dog as our child! She gets birthday cards and pressies,' said Julie, 29.

'I come from a Catholic family and now that we are married I know my grandparents are patiently waiting for us to announce a pregnancy,' said Louise, 32. 'My sister also gives me stern warnings about not getting sterilised because I'll change my mind.'

Raquel, 27, says she feels more self-imposed guilt than pressure. 'My mother is terminally ill and I feel as though I could have had a child so that she had grandchildren in her lifetime. Similarly, my family are the eldest grandchildren, and my Italian grandparents would love to see us producing their great-grandchildren. None of these things have ever been verbalised, but I feel them nevertheless.'

'My mother was initially disappointed,' said Fiona, 32. 'But now she watches my brother with his daughter and says: "You're right – don't do it!"'

Rachel, 37, said that she was 'very clucky at 26 or 27 years of age' and would have had a child but was not in a relationship at the time. 'All that changed at 30 when I had a serious car accident,' she said. 'Our fathers were the only ones [who] were disappointed. Our mothers understood exactly!'

Susan J. & David L. Moore

Ros, 45, has been in a de facto relationship for 25 years, and says that throughout the time that she has been with her partner they have been expected to produce offspring. 'There's always remarks like: "Oh you'll have to get married when you have kids." As the years have passed they came to think that we couldn't make babies – until we informed them that we had chosen to be child-free. Even after I was sterilised my Mum still said: "Oh don't worry, you can still adopt".'

If young women feel pressured today, life was much harder for women deciding 20, 30 or 40 years ago.

'I was very pressured to have a family,' said Sally, 51. 'My parents were a major source of pressure and so were my brothers and brothers-in-law. My father said: 'Who's going to have the children of the next generation?'' in a loud aggressive voice, as if nobody else would if I didn't. My mother was always pointing out darling little children's clothes in the shops. Friends seemed to think I was a freak for not having children.'

Luckily there are also many families who are very supportive.

Many years after Genevieve and her husband took their private decision, they discussed it with their parents, who were very understanding. 'Last year Anthony's parents visited us. We were getting dinner ready – the table was set, the candles were lit, the mood music was on – and his mother just turned to me and said that she really understood our decision not to have children. There was a sense of peace, a real sense of intimacy. There were no children crying, wanting to be fed, waiting to be bathed…just us, talking, reminiscing, planning. I believe she really did understand,' said Genevieve.

Anne has never experienced pressure from her family. 'My older sister married long before me, didn't want and didn't have children, so the precedent was set for me. Four years after her marriage a medical condition precluded her from producing a child – she was relieved. We both travelled a lot and did interesting things, so no one pestered us to have children. My parents both died when I was 29 or 30, but had never pressured me anyway.'

Prepare to justify yourself

Women are often the harshest critics of the child-free. Many mothers take a woman's decision not to have children as a direct criticism of their own choice and lifestyle. They may become very defensive when a woman says she will not be having children.

A parent would rarely be asked 'Why did you have children?' or 'When are you going to stop having children?', but non-parents are often asked 'Why don't you have children?' or 'When are you going to start a family?'. It is assumed that parenthood is an inevitable, natural part of every person's life and as such is not open to question.

'I am sick of trying to justify my decision to people planning to breed – and it is impossible to have a reasonable argument with these people,' said Fiona, 32.

Julie, 37, says she has a repertoire of standard answers for people who continually ask her if she'll change her mind, including: 'I would give it a go if I could buy a baby from Grace Bros and return it if I wasn't satisfied.'

William, 53, said he and his wife have felt pressured to have a family 'by piranha-like characters, usually female, who take it upon themselves to deem our relationship unfulfilled by the lack of children. Usually, these persons are easily disabused of their only idea with simple logic and logistics,' he said.

'I am asked a lot if I'm going to have children,' said Gayle, 36. 'The pressure comes from having to justify my decision to others. These "others" are usually women and either have or plan to have children. People tell me my choice is a shame because I would make an excellent mother. I'm sure I would too, but I just don't want to.'

Fiona, 41, says she has never felt pressure from family or male friends – only from female acquaintances. 'They cast aspersions on my fertility, make patronising assumptions and project their fears and insecurities through competitiveness and exclusion.'

'My closest friend wouldn't accept it for a long time,' said Sonia, 37. 'I think it's because she is so maternal. She wanted me to share her feelings, but now she accepts it.'

Kerri, 26, says that 'everybody else seems to be having children', while she still feels too young. 'I still don't really feel like a grown up at all,' she said. Kerri says the worst thing about not wanting children is her friends' negative attitudes towards her. 'All my friends think I will be too old by the time I want to,' she said. 'Everyone seems to believe that by the time I may or may not want children, it will then be too late, and that I will be too old once the child grows up.'

Tracie, 35, found that as life circumstances change, the pressure dropped off. 'Before I got married, everyone asked me when I was going to get married. When I was married, everyone asked when I was going to have kids. Now I'm older and in a live-in situation and have a divorce behind me, nobody dares ask anything so personal!'

'Friends who [are] having kids keep trying to convince me that I can't be "fulfilled", whatever that means, without children,' said Julie, 37. 'Once a pregnant friend spent over two hours telling me that I should get pregnant too so we could have babies together. That was a difficult one, I didn't want her to feel like I thought she was stupid or wrong just because I didn't want to do the same thing as she did. The funny thing is, I would never try to convince her that she should have a termination or remain childless. I wouldn't even think of it. I have theories about this pressure – could it be that those who have kids feel a bit shackled, maybe don't like or resent the way that we can come and go?'

John, 42, says that while male friends rarely comment on his child-free status, he has 'observed that a high proportion of our female friends at some stage express envy of our situation'.

Tracey, 39, owned a hairdressing salon for five years. Clients were always asking her when she would be having a family. 'One tends to get more pressure from people when in your thirties, 'cause they know the biological clock is ticking,' she said. 'And misery loves company, as they say!'

'I have a few patients who tell me that they pray for me to get pregnant! Especially Muslim and Italian men,' said Laura, a 41-year-old doctor. She says she has often discussed her decision with friends and family. 'The only time I feel a bit awkward about it is with friends who want kids but have failed, even with IVF. We don't introduce the topic because we don't have a soap box position on this and don't want to be "child-free bores".'

'Sometimes I get the old "So when are you going to settle down and have kids" thrown at me by friends who have children,' said Gabby, 32. 'My usual reply of "When hell freezes over" shocks some but most don't take me seriously. I'm as settled as I ever want to be at the moment.'

'Ostracism by society is a big drawback,' said Sally, 51. 'It's as if people with children don't want you to enjoy your child-free state. They are often very aggressive and hurtful with their comments.'

Many child-free people find themselves a group of like-minded friends and don't have to deal with pressure to have a family. Others say they simply don't care, and pressure does not bother them at all. Being child-free is simply more common and more acceptable now than even ten or 20 years ago, and some child-free people say they have experienced no pressure at all. A number of survey participants said they would not bring it up or discuss it with friends.

'My friends have been very much in agreement,' said Lyndall, 47, 'because a lot of them are also child-free, some by circumstance rather than choice initially, but now quite happy about it.'

'I think all our friends understand and respect our decision, the same as we respect theirs to have children,' said Helen, 33. 'I think there is a universally growing acceptance of being child-free.'

'All my friends and colleagues understand,' says Anne, a high school teacher. 'I'm a good communicator and able to explain what I mean. I also express my appreciation to the good friends I have who have had children. Someone has to do it.'

Sarah, 37, said that her friends know of her decision, but it isn't a subject they discuss a great deal. 'Of the two couples who are our closest friends, one couple cannot have children and do not want to go ahead with IVF treatment, the other couple cannot have children but have adopted a child. I feel that my husband and I should not flaunt our decision not to have children in front of couples who would love children but cannot have them.'

The media conspiracy

Can you think of a positive example of a child-free couple in advertising, films or television? Most childless couples are either planning to have a family or sad, weird old people.

'The constant barrage of media and political pressures irritates me, as though we are all meant to adhere to some corny "Hallmark Card" ideal,' said Betty, 47. 'It seems that producing a child or grandchild is in itself a cause for congratulations and recognition. For example, if a person is a victim of bad or good luck of some kind, the media will distinguish the individual as being a "mother of two" or "grandfather of six", as though this were something difficult to achieve, not the easiest and most common road taken.'

CHILD-FREE ZONE

The media doesn't like what it doesn't understand or can't explain. For example, a newspaper article about the 'anti-child' group called No Kidding! quickly descended into an attack on the child-free.

> Without resorting to Kennett-like exhortations, society should be reminded of the value of children, of their contribution to humanity (we'll call them 'clients' soon) even if it is just to remind the No Kidders that only children will work for $5.35 an hour serving short blacks on a Sunday afternoon.
>
> *Deirdre Macken,* Australian Financial Review, *14 August 1999*

Macken didn't give us any examples of the 'value of children' and their 'contribution to humanity', because providing examples would have removed the intangible emotional content from the argument. Every human has the potential to be of 'value' or to 'contribute'. Unfortunately just existing is not good enough. Macken goes on to say:

> The government could also deal with militant singles the same way it does with other minorities.
>
> Tell the No Kidders that society *will* educate their dogs for nothing. And reassure them Fido will be given all the skills required to look after them in their old age, when they need hip replacements and their food mashed up.
>
> If this doesn't work and the No Kidders begin demanding special leave from work for ping pong and pizza picnics, the governments of the world could grant them their own land.

All the No Kidders can go to an island somewhere, where they can sip cocktails in a splash-free pool and play mini golf without some brat walking across the green; where their slumber will only ever be broken by the sound of the sports master setting up water slides.

All the No Kidders can spend the rest of their lives in brat-free bliss. That should fix the problem in no time at all.

Well, at least we agree on the solution. Let's all go to that island! It sounds like a great place.

In this one article extract you can see many of the stereotypes and misbeliefs that the media imposes on the child-free. They are 'militant', 'single', a 'minority', they don't deserve the same time off as parents, they treat their dogs like children, they don't like splashing, they all belong to the café society and are the only people who don't like brats. Surely most parents would agree that 'brat-free bliss' is a desirable thing.

Think of the child-free couples you have seen in the movies and on TV. If you can actually think of any, you'll probably find that they were lonely, cold, weird or evil, like the couple who lived across the road from Samantha and Darren in 'Bewitched' or the Bundy's neighbours in 'Married with children'. They are usually the villains and end up losing out or 'coming around'. Now think of the most dysfunctional and annoying families on TV or in films. They always seem to be part of a happy ending.

For some reason the media want us to reproduce. Probably because they are simply frightened of offending the majority and watching their readership, box office takings or ratings drop. If aliens, ghosts, monsters and cars can be portrayed as friendly, why not child-free people? It's not so far fetched.

Health

There are three possible outcomes for the health of a woman who decides not to have children. Her health could be improved over all, it could be worsened, or it could stay the same. The same potential outcomes exist for a woman who does decide to have a child.

An individual can't know the future of their health. But with technology advancing at incomprehensible rates we now have a situation where we can make some predictions and have a statistical likelihood applied to the outcome. For example, many people are having genetic checks performed on both themselves, as potential parents, and their unborn child to determine the potential for genetic disorders and disease.

Technology is also giving us more choices for the future. Today's decisions can be undone by tomorrow's technology. Women can have children much later in life thanks to technology prolonging our lives and expanding the fertility window. One of the latest innovations is the 'ovary graft'. Ovary grafts are used to reverse premature menopause and counter the effects on fertility caused by some forms of cancer treatment. Vasectomies and tubal ligations are now readily reversible, provided they are done well in the first place. Reconstructive surgery is giving people back body parts that had been previously damaged beyond repair. This gives us more choice but also exposes us to more risk that must be factored into our decisions both now and in the future.

The best an individual can do for their future health is to make an informed choice today. To a large extent that is what this book is about – giving the individual the tools to make the decision that is right for them.

There are so many factors that affect our health that it is impossible to know precisely how *leaving out* just one factor may change the outcome of an individual's life.

Susan J. & David L. Moore

'As a non-child-rearing female I have had health problems – at least, the gyno said this,' said Christine, 39. Christine's gynaecologist, with the power of hindsight, must have some specific examples of how her health may have been affected. However, these problems weren't predicted or prevented.

There are people who believe that every once in a while you should take your car on to the open highway and really open it up. Burn out the gunk that builds up from the day-to-day city driving for which the car was *not* designed. Perhaps childbirth is seen as the gynaecological equivalent of this? There is apparently a condition resulting from a build up in the uterus as a result of having too many periods without a pregnancy. After all, humans weren't designed to live this long without following the evolutionary imperative. But then again, how many cars have performed well during the day-to-day commute only to break down 20 minutes into the freeway drive? We've become used to a different way of life.

While many child-free women are concerned about the long-term affects of the contraceptive pill, the jury seems to be out on this. Certainly when we raised this question with a GP, as we were concerned about using the pill for a long time without a break, it was dismissed as a negligible concern. But the question continues to be asked and we believe quite rightly so. Doctors don't have all the answers. If the pill were the perfect solution to the contraception problem, we wouldn't still be working on different answers. More male contraceptive options are on the way. But it is likely that men won't be trusted and women will still take the pill for its beneficial side effects.

There have been studies that point to an increased risk of breast cancer in women who do not have children. However, the risk is apparently greater for women who have children later in life than for those who have none at all. Many other risk factors need to be taken into account as well, such as family history, breastfeeding and cigarette smoking.

Some less obvious issues that may impact on a person's health include the first pregnancy after coming off the contraceptive pill. We have known several people - and apparently this is quite common - who have had miscarriages in this situation. The physical damage can be examined, but the mental trauma perhaps not so easily.

There is no conclusive evidence that not having a child will cost you your health in the long run. However, there are plenty of identifiable hazards that need to be addressed before embarking on the path to parenthood. The one thing that everyone agrees upon is that happiness is a key component to healthiness.

Discrimination in the workplace

It is an unfortunate but recognised fact that pregnant women are frequently discriminated against in the workplace. Women of child-bearing age may also be discriminated against simply because pregnancy is a possibility. It is often still assumed that once a woman marries, it is only a matter of time before she will leave her job to start a family. The discrimination shows when the company does not invest in her training and development or consider her for promotion. The problem is as rife in small business as it is in large corporations. While women in undergraduate courses at university now outnumber men of the same age, in postgraduate courses such as the Masters of Business Administration (MBA) men outnumber women. These courses are often very expensive and tend to be funded by employers.

We participated in a talkback radio program called 'Life Matters' on Radio National (RN) with economist Tom Nankivell. Tom related the story of himself and a colleague being offered subsidised study by their employer. The colleague, with a family and a mortgage, received full pay while he studied. However, Tom only received half pay. According to Tom it was quite clear that he was being discriminated against because he didn't have a family and a mortgage, but it was 'hushed up around the office'.

Susan J. & David L. Moore

The term 'family man' has positive connotations in business. In very traditional and conservative companies such as law firms, men with a wife and family may be seen as more responsible and committed. A male CEO or managing director with children somehow seems friendlier. Anecdotal evidence tells us that some are promoted ahead of their single or child-free colleagues. A male politician with a wife and children at his side is portrayed as more trustworthy – surveys have pointed to NSW Premier Bob Carr's lack of children contributing to his image problem – especially with women voters. (Carr's wife Helena is a successful businesswoman.)

There is often an assumption that child-free people can work longer hours than colleagues with a family. It is seen as responsible and understandable that the working mum leaves at 5 o'clock every day to collect her small child from day care, but anyone else who leaves on time to go to the gym or meet friends is 'not putting in a full day's work'.

If a woman is sometimes considered less committed to her career once she has children, the woman without is often considered so committed to career that she has no life outside work and is able to do far more than her fair share.

Jenny Hulme in New Woman, *January 1995*

For Jill, a 32-year-old publications manager, having no children means 'more opportunities but can lead to an expectation of no family commitments and therefore an expectation of putting more hours in'.

'Work thinks we can do shit hours because we haven't got children to go home to,' said Stephanie, a sales assistant.

Tracie, a 35-year-old ranger, finds that the topic of kids rarely comes up in her work environment. 'I am in a job where women are very much in the minority, so I feel I am setting a precedent anyhow.'

'Even the veterans in the hospital where I worked put pressure on me of a very insidious emotional kind,' said Sally, 51.

'There is more pressure at work, because employers only expect more,' said Sue, 35. 'They tend to forget you still have family and responsibilities, although you don't have children. I sometimes also feel they don't take your career plans seriously because they believe you're going to eventually "run off" to have a family.'

Some of Genevieve's work colleagues quite clearly stated their expectations that she would start a family. 'I remember one man I worked with actually bet me $20, in a friendly way, that I would start a family in the next three years. I left that workplace before I could collect the $20!'

Genevieve is now 39, has completed an MBA and works as a professional speaker. 'When I was first employed by a very large company, I was asked as part of the interview when I would be starting a family. This was my first position in the workforce, and I was only 22 years old, so I answered honestly. The question is, of course, against EEO (Equal Employment Opportunity) principles and I would respond differently now.'

In general Ana, a psychologist, thinks that being child-free will present her with more possibilities, but she is concerned that 'some employers will discriminate, and I will miss getting hired or promoted [because they believe] I may have children in the future.'

Dealing with contraception, sterilisation and abortion

It can sometimes be difficult to obtain sterilisation if you are childless. Many doctors are unwilling to perform the operation on childless men and women, as they so often see people who want to reverse the procedure. It becomes easier to obtain when you are older, but by then a woman may have been using contraceptives for over 20 years.

'I have considered [sterilisation] but have not found a doctor willing to perform the procedure,' said Helen, 33. 'We are from New Zealand and at age 25 I asked my doctor about it. He refused to discuss it until I was 30. At 30 I approached him and he said 35! I persisted and he checked a few specialists who said no – as apparently they can be sued if I were to change my mind. If I don't know my own mind at 30, I'm not sure when I will. What really riled me was that they said my husband could have a vasectomy but I couldn't have my tubes tied. I did not want this as I would not want to ruin my husband's chances if anything happened to our relationship.

'I am the one who definitely does not want children. He also doesn't want them but I don't think he feels as strongly about it as I do. It doesn't cause any strain, but I think he would easily change his mind if married to someone else who wanted them.'

'I don't understand why I should have to undergo psychological analysis ten times first, when there are no such requirements for becoming a parent,' said Sue, 29.

'I have often thought of vasectomy,' said Chris, 28. 'But I believe that [for the] childless… under 30 it is near impossible to get a doctor in Australia to perform that operation.'

'I wanted to be sterilised as soon as I found out it existed,' said Julie, 37. 'But no one would do it. I believe that they – the doctors and clinics – thought that I didn't know what I was on about. I was told that, unless I had kids, they wouldn't do anything until I was 35. I thought it was very unfair. But my ex-husband got sterilised so that helped.'

CHILD-FREE ZONE

Pauline is a 55-year-old mental health nurse. In her late twenties she approached several doctors requesting a tubal ligation. 'Most doctors refused on the grounds that I would change my mind and perhaps sue them. When I was 30 I became pregnant and sought a termination through [the Family Planning Association's] Pre-term [clinic]. Only then was I allowed a ligation. I wonder if fewer obstacles are put before women making that decision now?' Pauline's sister was later diagnosed with schizophrenia, and she feels that her position made it easier for her sister to have the operation.

Jan, 57, a registered nurse and medical secretary, asked to be sterilised in her twenties. 'The doctor asked me to wait in case we changed our minds. Finally when he considered we were certain, I was 31 and the doctor was my boss and friend. There may be others who would not have performed the procedure at that time.'

However, other people report that it is not hard to find a doctor who will perform the operation. You simply need to keep trying until you find one, or lie and say you have three children. The alternative for child-free women is to take the contraceptive pill for years, or use a form of contraception that is less safe or has a higher failure rate.

Normajeane is 34 and has been married for almost thirteen years. 'I never wanted to have kids and luckily my husband was happy to oblige by getting a vasectomy after our first year of marriage. He was only 23 at the time but we didn't have the trouble that we thought we would convincing a doctor to do so. Our GP said that he wouldn't do it but referred us to a specialist who, although not keen to, said that he had been approached by many others like us and would prefer to do it himself in a way that would be reversible than have us go elsewhere. When we saw the specialist I had to undergo an intense personal psychological interrogation. After I had satisfied his curiosity, he turned to Grant and said "Don't want kids, mate?". Grant said "Not really" and that was it! I don't think that it is fair to expect a woman to take the pill for up to 30 years, God knows what that could do to your body! And let's face it, nothing else is foolproof.'

Susan J. & David L. Moore

'When I was 37, I had my tubes clipped,' said Lorraine, 52. 'This had a rather interesting effect as it seemed to lift a great weight off my shoulders. Although I had not felt consciously 'guilty' about not having a child, now it seemed that feeling was gone now it was now longer possible to be pregnant. All to do with my mother's vibes!'

At 23 years of age, Lyn, now 44, decided that 'taking contraception for the next 30 odd years was ridiculous' and set about finding a doctor who would perform a tubal ligation. 'It is something that I have never regretted,' she said. 'In fact I list it as one of my greatest achievements.

Genevieve, 39, took the pill for sixteen years until her husband had a vasectomy in 1993. 'It's fascinating and frustrating to us that about six years after we were married we went to a specialist to ask about Anthony having a vasectomy, and the specialist refused. He said we were too young to make up our minds on such a major issue. So that meant I stayed on the pill for several more years until we were "old enough" to know our own minds, to make an "informed decision"!'

'I thought I would find it difficult finding a doctor who would perform the operation so my first port of call was Family Planning. I asked if they could send me to a sympathetic doctor, and had absolutely no problems. The doctor they sent me to asked lots of questions about why and so on. I must have convinced him because at the end of the interview he agreed to perform the tubal ligation the following week.'

'I'm going to the GP tomorrow to get a referral to the urologist for a vasectomy,' said Roger, 35. 'It's my 35th birthday present to my wife. I hope to have it done this month some time.'

CHILD-FREE ZONE

'I accidentally fell pregnant twice and had terminations both times,' said Julie, 37. 'It felt like my body had been invaded by an alien. I needed no post-termination counselling and both times left the clinic walking on air. It was a huge relief.'

Fiona reports a similar sense of relief. 'While I have tried to be responsible with contraception throughout my adult life, mistakes happen (and have, twice) and I am 41. So obviously, being pregnant didn't change my mind – I was very quick to terminate both pregnancies. Even now, years later, I remember my fear and horror at being pregnant, and the utter relief after the abortion.'

'I have had two unplanned pregnancies, the last with my ex-partner of ten years, and had no hesitation in terminating this pregnancy,' said Janelle, 33. 'I believed that my partner had no right to influence my decision, and gave him no reason to think so. I was fortunate that he respected me enough to leave the decision to me.'

'Health problems over the last six months make sterilisation a real possibility for me,' said Christine, 39. 'This is fine by me, but doctors are reluctant, even though I have made it very clear that I don't need a uterus.'

'I asked my family doctor when I was around 20 and he fell off his chair! Of course he would not consider it then. Said I had to be married, which will probably never happen,' said Fiona, a solicitor in a de facto relationship. 'I have had numerous gynaecological problems, so I'd consider having the whole thing removed and displaying it on my bookshelf.'

'I feared I was pregnant when I was 35 and the possibility of having an abortion made us consider and decide on sterilisation,' said Ros. 'It was my decision to have my tubes tied ten years ago. My partner was with me. It has been liberating not to have to think about any other forms of contraception since! I wanted to make sure that I never conceived, and the best way was to have my tubes tied. Many girlfriends said: 'Why didn't you make him do it?" The fear of testicular cancer together with the above reason is why.'

Lyndall, 47, decided on sterilisation following an ectopic pregnancy, due to having an IUD inserted. 'I had also previously conceived with a diaphragm and had problems of depression with the pill,' she said. 'At 28 I was lucky to find a gynaecologist who would do it. I was not in a relationship at the time. I had clips, which is supposedly reversible. I have never regretted that decision.'

'At one point, my paranoia about being too fertile led me to insist on the pill, a condom and spermicide! I really didn't want children. However, I doubt that I would go to those extremes again,' said Raquel, 27.

Anne says she may have considered sterilisation if she'd married younger. 'If my dear husband had lasted longer than the two years he lived after we were married, I couldn't say. I'd never quite decided to do it earlier, in case I'd met someone for whom children were very important. For them, I would have liked to keep the choice available.'

The stereotypes

By far the biggest complaint of child-free people is that they are tired of being told they are selfish.

The stereotype of the child-free as cold, selfish people who dislike children, overload their pets with affection and grow old, bitter and lonely is just that – a stereotype which does not reflect reality. Like parents, most child-free people are warm and enthusiastic individuals who give of themselves in other ways.

CHILD-FREE ZONE

Some of the more common assumptions include:

- Child-free people come from broken families and had unhappy childhoods.

- Child-free women are neurotic career bitches.

- Child-free men are immature and irresponsible.

- Child-free people hate children.

- Child-free people have 'child substitutes' such as a pet or a younger partner.

Stephanie, 36 is annoyed that she and her husband are 'classed as child-haters (when we're not). We love them,' she said. 'Friends kids and godchildren are great fun and you get to hand them back at the end of the day.'

'As a nanny I have come into contact with a lot of children, and generally, I like them,' said Anaïs, 38. 'Seeing them go from babies through the different stages of development is very interesting.'

Lori, 42, says that she and her husband were 'prejudged as selfish, self-absorbed, not having Christian values, not liking children and being eccentric'.

'Oh and by the way, my childless friends and I have far fewer pets than our child-rearing friends!' wrote Trudi.

The only common thread among survey respondents is that, in general, most are keen to make something interesting of their own lives while not imposing on other people.

Susan J. & David L. Moore

Missing out

People who have decided not to have children understand that they will miss out on many experiences that parents have. These include good and bad experiences.

'You definitely miss out on another dimension, emotionally and socially,' said Maureen, 43.

Kerry, 36, saw a possible negative to remaining child-free as 'not to have had the experience physically and not feel the love that some people do for their children'.

'The occasional stirring in my loins when I see a dad having a good time with [his] kid causes a bit of grief, and growing old alone sometimes freaks me out,' said Chris, 28, who recently separated from his wife, partly because she wanted children.

Alan, 46, says he will miss 'not teaching a child how to play my sports – golf, skiing, tennis, swimming'.

Heather, 32, feels that while she is not missing out, as she helped raise her husband's (now adult) children, her parents may be missing out. 'I sometimes feel sad for my parents as I know they would enjoy grandies and sometimes I feel that I should be having babies, but I feel that when I weigh everything up the decision is not to.'

However, older survey respondents for whom child-bearing was no longer an option generally felt that they had not 'missed out' on anything, and that they had only gained from remaining childless. They have no regrets.

Irresponsible breeding (the 'stupidity vortex')

At the risk of offending many, there is a growing and popular belief that poorer, less educated and less intelligent people are having more children than their well educated, middle class counterparts. Those with higher incomes are opting not to have children, or to limit their family to one or two children whom they can afford to raise while maintaining their careers and lifestyle as much as possible.

Peter McDonald in *Families in Australia* (1995) predicts that a high proportion of women will have no children and that one child families will become more common. Professional women with higher education, he says, are the most likely to defer marriage, and children and often bypass them completely.

The growing 'underclass' in Australia is a fact, with welfare organisations left trying to solve the problems created by the poverty trap. The promotion and funding of birth control to lower socio-economic groups is seen by many as one way to lower the birthrate.

Susan Faludi, in her book *Backlash: the undeclared war against American women* (1991), found that media campaigns persuaded women to address the 'birth dearth' and save the race from outbreeding by less desirable members of society.

While our sample of survey respondents is not large or random enough to draw any conclusions about this, it was a popular theme in their comments.

'My dad, the original "continue the gene pool guy", often tells me "we need to outbreed the whackers",' said Anne, 26. 'While condescending, the phrase illustrates the concerns of people our parents' age who have experienced the development from the quiet

1950s to a world full of non-working 'whackers'. "We didn't have whackers back then", he says. "The world pays them to breed."'

'I find most children to be very badly behaved,' said Tracie, 35. 'Of course I blame the parents. I strongly believe the wrong people are having children. I have few doubts that I would be a good parent, but I would not want my child mixing with the kids around today.'

'My biggest concern is probably that those of us who think about it are not having kids, while poverty and abuse seem to be the only future for too many innocent children of parents who didn't think about their responsibilities,' said Lyndall, 47.

'I strongly believe that there are far too many people who should not have children for a myriad of reasons,' said Lorraine, 52.

The best outcome we can hope for from this book is for more people to *think* before deciding to have children. A frightening number of people neither think about it nor make an active decision – they just have children.

The worst reasons for having a child

Normajeane, 34, wrote in a letter to us: 'As for being selfish, I have heard every selfish reason under the sun for having children – "Who's going to look after you when you're old?", "I want someone who will love me unconditionally", "Who's going to continue the family name?", "I wanted to give every one of my boyfriends his own child" (this was from a woman who was on welfare and had six children from about four different men), "Look at the joy we get from them", "I want a grandchild", "I thought my boyfriend would marry me if I got pregnant", "It was an accident", "My biological clock is ticking". Are there actually any selfless reasons for giving birth? How can the words "I want" be considered less selfish than the words "I don't want"?'

Kate, 55, thinks that women decide to have children far too easily. 'For many it's like buying a pet,' she said. 'If you ask them why they did it, it's not a pretty answer, and many regret doing so.'

Karena, 45, agreed. 'All the pluses that sprint to mind, as related to me by parents, on examination seem vaguely selfish: having an "image" of oneself; a "tribe" of your own; people who will always love you (not necessarily!); the satisfaction of moulding another human being (what a power trip). Most parents seem to spend all their time complaining to me then telling me I made the right decision.'

One of the worst reasons to have a child came from Raquel, 27, whose 'misogynist ex-boyfriend' told her that 'every man wants children. They are a reflection of one's self. You'll have a hard time finding a husband if you let that particular opinion out of the bag'.

As many people who create more of themselves are subconsciously aware that it may be a mistake, they can't give their true motivations. We need to translate their rationalisations.

Rationalisation	Translation
To carry on the family name	Trying to please Dad
I just love children	Out of touch with inner child and existing children
I want my kids to have all the things I didn't	Unfulfilled childhood desires and fantasies
We'd like to try for a boy/girl this time	Gender identity insecurity. Disappointment with existing progeny
I want someone to visit me when I'm old	Has a fear of aging and an exploitative personality
We want to give our parents grandchildren	Still seeking parental approval
I have superior human genes	An oxymoron

<u>Source:</u> – Voluntary Human Extinction Movement – www.vhemt.org.

In this chapter, we have compiled a list of poor reasons to start a family.

To save a marriage

When both men and women are experiencing so much uncertainty about their emerging roles, there is some comfort to be drawn from the fact that the role of 'parent' is unequivocally defined. This is potentially hazardous: it sometimes means that children are being used by one or both parents as a kind of emotional crutch to compensate for the breakdown of intimacy between spouses.

Hugh Mackay in Reinventing Australia, *(1993)*

It should seem obvious that having a child does not bring a couple closer together. In fact, the opposite may occur, where one partner feels resentful, neglected or increasingly alone. An event as significant and stressful as having a child becomes one of those 'make or break' opportunities. Where a marriage is already fragile, having a child is more likely to be what 'breaks' it. With 54.2% of divorces in 1991 involving children, it is certainly worth thinking about this possibility *before* starting a family.

Our divorced survey respondents were lucky enough to realise this before having a child. Some have had to cope with raising children from a partner's previous marriage, while not having children of their own.

'[Not having children] was my decision, but he went along with it,' said Jane, 48,of her ex-husband. 'A couple of times when things were rough he asked if I wanted a child, and I would not have one in the hope of saving a marriage.'

A study of post-natal depression in men and women by RMIT University in Melbourne showed that poor relationships can be a factor in the condition. RMIT Professor of Women's Health, Carol Morse, said that the quality of a relationship between partners was a major predictor for post-natal depression and an inability to cope with a child. 'Partnerships that are in trouble or of poor quality before pregnancy are going to be further strained by the arrival of the baby,' she said.

Men often feel that they have been somehow 'replaced' by the child and that their partner no longer considers their needs. They report an increasing feeling of working simply to survive and not having control over their existence.

Women often feel resentful that the burden of child-rearing and an increasing share of other household duties now rests solely on their shoulders. A 1998 Australian National University study found that once women became mothers, they were twice as likely to do the cleaning, shopping, ironing, washing and meal preparation. As a woman's responsibility increases, the level of sharing decreases. Although there was more sharing in the households where women work, there remained a clear 'second shift' for most women, and especially for working women with children. Men were much more likely to have access to job benefits such as sick leave, holiday leave, flexible hours, long service leave, carer's leave or use of a company car, but unlikely to take advantage of these perks to care for children.

While having a child may not be *bad* for a healthy relationship, the claim that it will save an already shaky one is quite obviously false.

To beat the biological clock

Women in their late thirties and early forties are often gripped by a blinding realisation that if they don't have a child soon, it will be too late. This sudden fear compels many to rush out and get pregnant so they don't miss out on what everyone tells them is 'a wonderful experience that is not to be missed'.

'The concept of the biological clock terrifies me,' said Raquel, 27. 'I don't want a surge of hormones over-riding my rational reasons for making the decision not to have children.'

CHILD-FREE ZONE

G.H., 42, said that her 'biological urge is strong – there is a sense of guilt and of having missed "something"'. However, she says she is unlikely to change her mind now that her 'biological clock is just about out of time'.

The problem is, while they may be financially and perhaps emotionally more stable, older people tend to be set in their ways and less willing to accept the natural changes that having a child brings. As well as joy, the child may well bring regrets and resentment. If you have any sense of doubt, don't do it. There are other ways to enjoy the company of children. Take part in an 'aunties and uncles' program, take an interest in your friends' children and offer to look after them, or get involved as a tutor in your field of expertise.

Many child-free women report that they have never felt a 'maternal urge'. To them it would seem that the biological urge is to have sex, not make babies. The older people in our survey group don't regret not having children, as their lives have been filled with other rich and varied experiences.

'I have never felt a maternal moment in my 43 years,' said Kathryn. 'And if I do, I prefer to have a cat or a dog.'

'I don't have much time left, but my heart tells me if you're in any kind of doubt – don't do it!' said Kerry, 36.

'I don't believe in the biological urge or imperative,' wrote Kate, 55. 'I believe the impulse is society driven, because so many people stand to gain.'

'My mother tells me lately that my hormones are talking and it's time to be a mother, however, I can't hear them,' said Leanne, 34.

Fiona, 32, reports having 'not even a spark' of maternal instinct, especially to very young children, towards whom she has 'no feeling towards at all. They even smell funny to me'.

It is a common and insulting view that 'biology is destiny' and that child-free women are not fulfilling their 'natural' role. Childless women are no less 'women' than their sisters with children – whether they are unable to have children or simply choose not to.

When you approach the age when having children will soon no longer be an option, stop and take stock of what you have. Are you happy, is your life full enough without having your own children? If the answer is yes, why have a child just in case you may feel you've missed out on something?

To provide security in your old age

The era has gone where children were a kind of insurance policy on your income, and that more children meant more people to help you out in your old age.

Although taxes paid by working citizens finance many systems of providing support for retired citizens, the concept of needing younger people to support older people is obsolete. Social security systems are artificial and can be adjusted for changes in society, such as the number of workers.

There are better investments to ensure a comfortable retirement. The introduction of compulsory superannuation was partly intended to ensure that people have money for their retirement so they don't rely on government handouts. The implication being that many people don't plan well for their retirement. Despite this, it is well documented that people who don't have children are financially independent earlier than those who do.

'Some people have said 'who will look after you when you're old?'' said Kathryn, 43. 'I think this is the most selfish reason to have children as most people tend to spend less time with their parents as they get older. It is surely a selfish reason also as the child should be free to enjoy their life and parents should put no expectations on their children.'

CHILD-FREE ZONE

Anaïs, 38, said: 'Having children is no guarantee they will be willing to look after you later on.'

Greedy children are more often seeking to inherit from their parents than give anything back to them. A recent attempt at changing nursing home legislation in Australia to an up-front payment system brought outrage from some of the children of people moving into nursing homes. One woman on television proclaimed how tragic it was that her mother would have to sell her home to be able to afford to move into a retirement village with appropriate care. While there is little doubt that there were genuine problems with the scheme, it was obvious that in this case what she really meant was that it was tragic that her mothers' assets would not be passed on to her.

Surely the reason you work towards owning your own home is to have financial security in your old age when you are no longer able to earn an income, not to pass wealth on to greedy children so that they do not have to work towards their own financial security in retirement.

'I often hear people say: "Who's going to look after you in old age?"' said Fiona, 32. 'Funny thing is, the people who say this are not looking after their parents.'

Children cannot be relied upon for company either. In fact, it has been said that elderly people living with their children are among the loneliest in society. How many people do you know who live many miles away from their parents, often interstate or overseas? The population is more mobile than ever, and children offer no guarantees.

'With nine children in my family, only one of them lives within two hours' drive of my parents,' said Helen, 33. 'My mother died last year and now my father struggles on alone. Having nine children didn't seem to do them much good in their old age. That to me must be the most selfish reason to have children – to have someone to care for you in your old age.'

'Friends say I'll be sorry when I'm old,' said Tracey, 39. 'They say I'm selfish now and I'll suffer for that later. I say, they're selfish for having kids in the hope that the kids will be there for them when they're old. I think it would be worse to have kids and be rejected or ignored by them when you're old, than to have no one at all. You don't miss what you haven't had.'

'After all, I don't visit my parents regularly nor support them, so why would ours visit us?' said Kim, 40.

Many people believe that because their parents made the decision to have them, it is the parents who owe the children every advantage in life. 'If you don't like the way your children behave or live their lives, then perhaps you shouldn't have had them, or at least [should have] thought harder about the consequences before you did.' There have *never* been any guarantees.

Usually the children have grown up, been set free, and made full lives of their own. They may be unable to help their parents even if they want to.

Your parents want grandchildren

Have you ever pondered why your parents exhorted you to give them grandchildren? The answer: revenge. Triumphantly you hand them the bundle that contains, unequivocally, the most beautiful baby ever produced. They hand it back. 'Now you will find out what you put us through!' they chortle maniacally, running like the clappers towards the horizon.

Felicity Biggins in The Australian, *30 January 1996*

CHILD-FREE ZONE

Older people often experience social pressure to have grandchildren. All some people seem to do is talk about their grandchildren. Many parents place considerable pressure on their children to produce offspring. One friend's Mum even knitted an entire suitcase full of baby clothes for her future grandchild, who has so far failed to materialise.

Chris, 28, says his Mum is pretty keen for grandchildren and 'just says things, never directly but insinuated'.

However, as we were once told, the main reason they want you to have grandchildren is so that you can suffer as they have.

There is no reason why your parents can't be surrogate grandparents for other kids. Dad was keen on grandchildren but knew that we were unlikely to 'produce', so he enjoyed the company of friends' children from the country. They would come to stay, make things for him to stick on the fridge and generally gave him a lot of pleasure. Other would-be grandparents could consider getting involved at their local school helping with a reading group or sports teams. With divorce on the rise, there are many volunteer community groups that match surrogate grandparents with kids who don't have any of their own.

'The most amusing thing my mother ever said to me just after she heard that my partner's mother had been diagnosed with cancer [was]: "I'm sure she's thinking about her mortality and would just love you to give her a grandchild"' said Trudi, a writer and illustrator.

'My parents frequently bring the issue of "their grandchildren" up,' said Brian, 36. 'My mid-thirties brother does not have a stable relationship from which they will get the next generation. Dad just wants the family name to continue, Mum wants someone to knit and sew for and to dote over.'

When it comes down to it, no matter what you feel you don't 'owe' your parents, it's your life to do with as you please.

Susan J. & David L. Moore

To live vicariously through your children

A person who feels that their life is unsuccessful or that they have not fulfilled their dreams may try to live their life again through their child. The positive side to this is parents who simply want to present their children with opportunities that they did not have themselves while growing up. The negative version is the parent who pushes the child towards achieving *their* dreams and not the child's own dreams.

One of the more obvious examples of this is the 'stage mother', who drags her young daughter to ballet and singing classes every Saturday, when the girl would rather be swimming or reading or simply playing with her friends. The saddest thing about it is that transferred ambition rarely works. The daughter may end up graceful but resentful and still unsuited to a career on the stage. Similarly there are 'netball mums' and 'rugby dads', forcing their child to do something they are quite obviously neither interested in nor good at.

Child-free people often feel quite strongly that they have to make a difference themselves.

'People who have children often see that as their contribution to the future,' said Fiona, 41. 'Maybe those of us who don't have children have to work harder to leave that lasting effect, into the future.'

'Being child-free gives me the opportunity to develop myself within, rather than through another human being,' said Janelle, 33.

'My skills are not restricted to reproducing and having those children make a difference to the world,' said Genevieve, 39. 'I trust that I can make that difference on my own. If I can help myself and other individuals then my life has really been worthwhile. That is what I will leave the world when I am gone – and I trust my impact will not have to wait until I am gone.'

To get attention or belong

Sad as it may be, the two occasions when a woman is assured of being the centre of attention and showered with gifts is when she gets married and when she has a baby. A number of our respondents reported they have friends who admitted having a child to get the attention and love of a parent. Others wanted to become part of the 'mothers' club' social circle, as all their friends were mums and they felt left out and unimportant.

'My sister fell pregnant accidentally (she's 29) and since her baby was born I rarely ever hear from my Mum. I know it's because she is preoccupied with her granddaughter. I can't help feeling that she is disappointed with me. Our big family get-togethers are mildly sickening – all these clucky women coo-cooing over the babies as though they are the most important things in the world,' said Marianne, 31.

Although many conceptions are unintended, conformity is probably the number one cause of wanted pregnancies. Surprisingly, many who continue to have children have never considered doing otherwise. Most are reluctant to question tradition or appear different from what society considers normal. And when all your friends are doing it, it can be isolating to be the odd one out. In this situation, sadly, it looks like you'll need to find some new friends. With almost a quarter of Australian women now expected not to have children, it's not impossible to find some like-minded people.

To escape the realities of working life

Some women, feeling unfulfilled in their working life, see having a child as a way out. When you are slaving away in the office, working long hours for the average wage, it can be hard seeing your friends in the 'mothers' club' going to the gym, playing tennis or having lunch with the girls (albeit with toddlers in tow). Life as a homemaker suddenly starts to look attractive. The reality of motherhood is very different and unlikely to be a cure-all. Life as a new mum is not easy and most 'stay-at-home mums' will tell you that parenting is certainly a full-time job. Few families can afford not to have both partners working, and the woman may find that she then has two full-time jobs.

Sadly, the problem is part of a vicious circle. Women still tend to have less fulfilling jobs and less opportunities for advancement than men, partly because organisations are unwilling to invest time and money in female employees when their priority lies with having a family.

Sometimes, having one partner out of the workforce for an extended or indefinite period can cause strain on a relationship – due either to financial pressures or mild jealousy on the part of the working partner. Some friends of ours just had their third child. The father jokes that 'just when it becomes time for Robyn to go back to work, she has another baby'. Obviously they haven't worked out what causes babies yet, or the milkman still visits their area.

Medical scaremongering about the effects of delaying pregnancy

There has been some discussion in the media of studies that find an increased risk of breast cancer in women who do not have a baby. Others report that women who have a baby after the age of 35 are more at risk than those who have no children.

'[There is a] possible increased likelihood of breast cancer after sterilisation,' said Kate, 55.

It is important to put these findings into perspective and weigh up other risk factors in your life, such as genetic links, smoking or a high fat diet. Provided you live an otherwise healthy life and limit stress, you are at little greater risk than anyone else. There are also the negative effects of child-bearing and birth to consider, such as post-natal depression and gynaecological problems.

Some of our respondents expressed concern that there may be health risks, while others put it down to medical scaremongering.

To receive financial benefits

A friend's teenage sister in Tasmania desperately wanted to live out of home, but did not qualify for any financial assistance. She was able to live in a women's refuge temporarily by claiming that her mother mistreated her (a story our friend vehemently says is not true). She later became pregnant and decided to keep the baby on the basis that various one-off government payments and a single mother's allowance would allow her to live out of home while she studied.

While it may be rare for a person to have a child solely for the purpose of receiving more government benefits, the social security system does appear to encourage struggling families with one or two children to have more children in order to increase the payments they are entitled to. This is the result of so called 'family policy' and attempts to appease the 'average Australian' with election promises of more money. Poorly implemented social security policy encourages those people who can least afford it to reproduce.

Stuff a flamin' parrot! When are people going to start taking some responsibility for their own life and actions and stop expecting others to fund their life for them?

I'm referring to the article about the family with seven children (December 13), who claim they want public housing because their kids have to sleep on their grandparents' floor as they have no home.

Why don't they have a home? If you can't afford or don't want to save up a deposit on a home, then don't have seven kids and expect other taxpayers to give you one.

I lived with a wife and two children in a single garage for nearly a year so as we could save up a small deposit for our first home.

I've also suffered unemployment, but never did I expect my fellow Australians to pay for a home for me.

Plus, I restricted my breeding to two children. That way we could give them a fair education.

Letter to the Sun-Herald *in December 1998*

The Church tells me to

Religion is one of the most important factors in determining the size of families. Religious upbringing or pressure from family members can even influence women who do not think of themselves as religious.

So God created human beings, making them to be like himself. He created them male and female, blessed them and said 'Have many children, so that your descendents will live all over the earth and bring it under their control.'

Genesis 1.27–28

The Bible is full of references to having many children. Many people feel that the Church places a lot of pressure on them to reproduce. Those concerned with environmental or population issues are especially scathing. Marianne, 31, thinks 'the Catholic religion has a lot to answer for in their stance against contraception. The more people [who] are brought into the world, the harder stretched our natural resources become. Life is so cheap in other poorer countries'.

111

CHILD-FREE ZONE

Child-free people who belong to a church often find it extremely difficult to be honest about not wanting children. Other religious people sometimes see them as 'evil' or against Christian family values. A number of people admitted telling others that they were unable to have children, which invoked pity instead of anger.

'My mother thinks that if I have a child it will "fix me",' said Beth, 34. 'There is a strong Catholic tradition in our family, so each generation has had a nun for many years, who of course [doesn't] have children. So whilst not making that religious commitment I am just following in the footsteps of some of my ancestors!'

'The wedding vows in the Catholic Church always refer to the couple "accepting children lovingly from God",' said Sarah, whose husband comes from a large Catholic family. 'We left this out of our vows. No one has ever said anything to our faces about the omission, not even the priest who performed the wedding, however I always get the feeling that my husband's family had a good gossip about it.'

Sally, 51, is a retired scientist and now a writer who is proud to be leaving the world with '30 explicitly Christian short stories, two novellas and 100 poems'. She says she found the conflict difficult to cope with earlier in her life, and that the biggest problem has been other people's assumptions.

Luckily, more people now understand that being child-free — or gay or divorced or whatever else — does not make you any less 'Christian' than the next person, if that's where your beliefs lie.

Some people claim that their religious group needs more members to make the world a better place, but there's no guarantee that the offspring will follow the traditions of their parents. In fact, just the opposite seems to be the norm in modern societies. Besides, if the only people who will adopt a belief system are those born into it, there must be some serious flaws in that system.

Susan J. & David L. Moore

Your partner wants children

We think it is vitally important that you talk this issue over with your partner before it becomes an issue, and definitely before marrying.

You may know of men who went along with their partner's wishes to have a baby, and later took little interest in parenting. It happens the other way around too. A friend of ours loved children and wanted a family so much that his second wife, caught up in his excitement, finally agreed. She later admitted that she hated being pregnant, disliked being a mum and resented giving up her career as an airline steward. The marriage ended before the child was two years old, and now our friend hardly sees his son. It is often easier to go along with a partner's decision than rock the boat, but the consequences can be disastrous. The most difficult decision is to end a relationship where expectations differ on such an important issue as children.

'[It was a] personal decision which led to divorce as my partner wanted children,' said Stephanie, 41.

'My wife wanted children…we have separated now because of this, and a lot of other reasons,' said Chris, 28.

Children can be used as a tool for solving other problems in the home. The man who wants his wife to be home for him and cook his dinner, or who feels threatened by her career success, may encourage her to start a family to achieve his vision of domestic bliss. Equally, a woman who wants to 'trap' a man or make him pay more attention to her may see pregnancy as a way to do it.

'In my present de facto situation neither my partner nor myself have ever wanted children,' said Kathryn, 43. 'We had arrived at this decision before we got together. Both of us had been married before to partners who wanted children. I was married to a man eight years younger than myself. He wanted children but I never felt happy about him being a father. I felt he wanted them for all the wrong reasons and that ultimately I would be the main carer. Luckily we divorced, but this was a contributing factor to the breakdown in our relationship.'

Some child-free women feel that their decision may have been different if their partner had been firmly in favour of having a family.

'At a younger age I feared being influenced by a partner who really wanted kids,' said Lyndall, 47.

Giving in to a partner's desire to have children is not a recipe for a happy or equal relationship or a guarantee that you will change your mind.

To pass on the family name

If you are an only child and have no children you may understand what it feels like to be the 'end of the line'. It feels just fine. A little sad perhaps, when you have an unusual name or one with a certain history, but no big deal. Certainly not enough reason to produce offspring. Just think of that most famous of quotes — 'What's in a name?'

'To be honest I hardly remember my grandparents, so none of us has longevity unless we become "famous",' said Tracie, 35. 'I have a loyalty to my surname, but being female I don't feel I am ending my family line because if I had children I'd give them the father's name anyway.'

'I feel no desire to have descendants to "carry on the line",' said Anne, a high school teacher. 'Other family members, my cousins, have gone overboard this way. One had four kids, one has had eight children so far – it's downright irresponsible! The world is far too overpopulated already.'

'Truly, I find the concept of "leaving a child" to be interesting,' said Fiona, 32. 'I don't think I represent the sum of my parent's legacy –

I am a product of the life I have given myself, which may include something from my parents, but which is not my defining point.'

Carrying on the family name has long been an unquestioned justification for reproduction, but when you think about it, it's a slightly ridiculous one.

'I think people who believe in leaving "heirs" are small-minded and egotistical in their thinking,' said Lori, 42. 'What is important is how we live our lives and not what or who we leave to carry on.'

It was an accident

Surely one of the major benefits of living in the late twentieth century is the availability, in Australia at least, of a wide variety of contraception devices and access to safe abortions.

While mistakes can happen, is it fair for that mistake to turn into a child's life? The point is that we now have a choice, a *decision* to make as to whether or not to have the child. In the past, women simply did not have the means to prevent or terminate a pregnancy safely.

Gayle, a 36-year-old psychologist, says that an unplanned pregnancy would not affect her decision at all. 'I take precautions and complete responsibility to ensure I don't fall pregnant. If I did it would be an accident. I would not consider action other than an immediate termination. I was pregnant once – whilst using an IUD for contraception and terminated ASAP. I was 19 and a full-time student in a long-term relationship.'

It is true that contraceptives are not free from side effects, and not always cheap – and that if more women had been the medical researchers and legislators in the past, there almost certainly would be a safe and cheap contraceptive available right now. But at least we have the options available to us, and enough women are now in a position to be able to do something to further improve the situation.

Men who do not want children feel particularly vulnerable and not in control of their own destiny where they are unsure of their partner's stance on children. While most feel that they would stay in the partnership in the case of an unplanned pregnancy, a number say it would be grounds to terminate the relationship. Most quite rightly feel that they should not be bullied into having a family and that they should have equal decision-making power.

'Sometimes I even thought I would walk out of the marriage if [an unplanned pregnancy] had happened,' said Chris, 28. 'But I would have stuck it out, I think. That sounds like [a] justification [for] "all men are bastards".'

I am too clever and attractive not to pass on my genes

'Let's face it, most people have kids for their own reasons of vanity and self-interest anyway,' said Kerry, 36.

You might think you and your partner are highly intelligent and beautiful human beings who would produce wonderful children that would be a gift to the world. This may be true, but perhaps the 'large ego' gene is not a good one to be passing on. The sad reality is that there is no guarantee what your children will be like. A child is not necessarily the sum of its parents' traits. No one has to pass a minimal intelligence test in order to qualify for a license to have children.

'I know the reason I'll end up having kids is to raise great minds, and with his sporting genes, a great sportsman,' read one letter received from a bright young professional woman. What if the child had her sporting genes and his mind? There are simply no guarantees.

Tracie's parents told her that 'there will be some great genes lost because of the people who are choosing not to have children'.

'I think children represent parents' fear of their own mortality,' said Kim, 40. 'In the end, you only live in someone else's memory and then only if it is a good recollection.'

When a couple says they want to have 'one of their own' they mean, 'make one that has our genes'. The mindset behind this bloodline mentality is deep and strong – it means more of 'us' and less of 'them'. It sounds a lot like racism. Throughout history wars have been fought on this thinking.

What IS a good reason for having children?

Are there any good rational reasons for having children? It is not often that you will hear someone being questioned as to why they decided to have kids. But decide not to have kids and everyone thinks it is their right to question you. Many survey participants pointed out that the question is just as valid in the positive as in the negative.

'No one has ever given me a good reason to have children,' said Kim, 40. 'It is always social or peer pressure or a mistake or whatever, but only once have I heard: "Well, I think I could raise some really good people."'

The truth is that most people who have a family have never considered doing otherwise. That means they did it for no reason at all. There was no decision involved.

'I fail to see that having children is any less selfish. I have yet to meet anyone who had planned a child, who didn't have it for the reason that "they" wanted a baby. Is that not selfish too?' said Helen 33.

Perhaps the funniest reason for having children came from Freud, who asserted that a woman's urge to have children stemmed from her lack of a penis. When you think of a child as a 'penis replacement', suddenly parenthood does seem a bit silly!

Susan J. & David L. Moore

Making the decision

The importance of discussing the issue of having children with your partner cannot be stressed enough. This should be done well before serious commitments are made so that expectations are set and disappointment and resentment can be avoided.

Problems in child-free partnerships occur when expectations differ, and one partner wants children less than the other. A couple may simply drift into buying a home, renovating it, changing careers and never actually discuss their longer-term expectations. It is also common for people to change their expectations when the prospect of no longer having a choice pushes many into parenthood.

'Originally it was a very personal decision about which I felt very strongly,' said Lorraine, 52. 'However, when I first met my husband and we discussed this, before marriage, I discovered to my delight that he felt the same way.'

Roger says that not having children was a joint decision with his then girlfriend, now wife. 'When Jacki and I were discussing moving in together, she said she would only move in if marriage were inevitable. She didn't want to end up a "common law" or de facto wife. Since we were basically deciding to get married, I came up with a list of topics to discuss, which included kids. I had had no desire for kids up to that point, so I wasn't getting married because it was time to procreate. I have never thought about the kid or no kid thing much before this, as I figured I would think about it once I was getting married. After discussing it, we both agreed that we didn't want children. So, officially we decided before she moved in and we got married six months later.'

'My partner wants children eventually but says he is okay with my decision,' said Gabby, 32. 'I made this decision long before we met and it was one of the first things I told him about myself and he still wanted a relationship. In years to come, if the subject of children comes up again, he can't say that I didn't forewarn him. It may sound selfish but I won't have a child to keep someone else happy.'

'I was married for sixteen years, he never wanted kids either and had a vasectomy at 22,' said Julie, 37. 'Since we separated, I have taken up with a man much younger than me, 22 years old, and he wants kids. Unfortunately he also sees me as a long-term prospect – eighteen months so far. He knows how it is for me but seems to think he will change my mind - ah the sweet optimism of youth! So far it's all fairly light-hearted – he talks about it, I grunt and switch on the TV.'

Jane, 48 used to worry about her ex-husband's 'heavy sexual demands' and did not know how she would cope with the additional burden of children. 'I was scared, worried how my husband would cope with reduced sex and finances. We did not really discuss it I suspect. He went along with what I said. It was my decision.'

Jan, 57, was married in 1962, at the age of 21 to John, then 24. She says they discussed children before getting married. 'We were fairly certain neither of us were enthusiastic about reproduction, but would not say a definite "no",' said Jan. 'However, it became evident during our first year of marriage that we did not want kids. It became a mutual agreement.'

Louise, 42, says she decided not to have children about 21 years ago, when her partner told her that he did not want children. 'I realised that I was more than comfortable with that and I realised I didn't either feel I had to have children or that I really wanted to,' she said.

While many women surveyed knew that they did not want children at an early age, most people seem to make a 'decision' much later.

Laura, a 41-year-old doctor, 'always assumed' she would not have children. 'In fact I requested a tubal ligation from the university health centre when I was 20 and of course was refused,' she said.

120

Susan J. & David L. Moore

'I decided not to have children when I was 12. I was determined to have a "choice". I decided again when I was 17, and had a termination after contraception failed. And forever after,' said Karena, 45.

'My decision was a personal one but one that has become a joint decision in the four years I have been with my partner,' said Tracie, 35. 'My partner and I have discussed this on occasion and I often tell him I hope he is being honest by saying he doesn't want children and not just fitting in with me. He says he's easy either way but would probably be a little disappointed if I suddenly decided I want children.'

Beth, 34, is living with a partner who is divorced and has two children from his first marriage. 'Turning 30 marked the time when I really thought that I would not bother to procreate,' she said. 'Turning 30 was significant for me in that, if I was going to have children I had always thought that I would be in the right relationship and working towards a family and future together already. I guess earlier than this I had always assumed that I would have children. Living with kids who have been through a nasty divorce and watching the problems this creates reinforces my commitment – I mean who plans to have this sort of thing happen?'

'I always thought one day I might feel maternal and want children, but I never did,' said Kathryn, 43. 'Only when I was married did the thought of actually having to confront this decision start to scare me. I would avoid discussing it which made me realise that I just couldn't see myself as a mother.'

John, 37, said he did not ever think about having children in detail. 'Since I turned 30 my feelings have waxed and waned to the extent of being quite against the idea altogether. I suppose in the last three years I have come to solidify the decision, however it has come about only through a deep understanding of my wife's feelings and the fact that we are fortunate to agree on such a big issue.'

CHILD-FREE ZONE

'The idea of not having children had been at the back of my mind for many years when I met my then wife-to-be,' said Brian, 36. 'It was not a conscious decision, so much as a revelation of unrecognised dislikes and fears. I was 24 years old at this time.'

'There was not any one given moment of decision,' said Sally, 51. 'My husband and I agreed in 1970, before we got married, that we didn't want children, but there were many moments of validation after that. I suppose the matter was finally decided in 1985 when I had a tubal ligation.'

The decision to remain child-free may not be a decision that is made only once. During the course of a relationship it may be made many times until there is a final acceptance that it is definite. There is always the possibility that expectations and goals may change, and as a result the issue of whether or not to have a family often needs to be an ongoing discussion.

'I am very definite that I do not want children,' said Genevieve, 39. 'However, Anthony, my husband, has wavered more than me. He is really great with kids, he is a hit with his nieces and nephews. He still has dreams about having children. However, the really important aspect is that we discuss all of this openly and honestly. We have discussed many, many times the advantages and disadvantages of having children. We are very honest with each other. I believe it is this degree of communication that has prevented the issue from having a detrimental effect on our relationship. For example, Anthony might say that he saw a friend with their child – and we talk about it. We discuss what the implications would be for us, on our relationship and on our freedom. We always reaffirm our decision, yet acknowledge that it is a major decision, and not one to be taken lightly.'

It's a matter of weighing up your life priorities. What do you want to do and achieve in your lifetime?

Susan J. & David L. Moore

Changing your mind

Most of the people surveyed were very firm in their decision not to have children. However, some are naturally reluctant to use the word 'never'.

'What of human nature is definite?' said Brian, 36. 'I don't know what the future holds, maybe hormonal changes, loss of spouse or a very heavy concussion! But at this point in time it would have to be something dramatic to cause that much of a change.'

'The only thing that would change my mind would possibly be if I was to become guardian after the death of somebody,' said Janelle, 33.

'At one point, when I was about 33 years old, I considered having a child, but my husband was firmly against it, so I didn't. I'm glad now that I didn't,' said Sally, 51. 'The period of strain in our relationship was not long lived. I decided that staying with my husband was more important to me than having a child.'

People who have decided not to have children will encounter many other people who are convinced that they will change their minds. Either a flash of insight will cause a sudden urge to reproduce, or they will be worn down by social and family pressure. Often the people telling us this will know nothing about us, but still feel they can dictate how our lives will be. It is insulting. However, it is possible that people unsure of their decision, one way or another, will be unfairly influenced by these interfering sorts. Factor them out of *your* decision.

We'd love to revisit our survey respondents in five to ten years to see how many have children then, but feel sure that most of them, who felt strongly enough about the issue to participate, will stick with their convictions.

What do child-free people do?

This is a silly question. Each child-free person is as different as each parent and can be found in an equally wide range of occupations, locations, leisure activities and social groups, if not more. The correct answer to this question might be 'anything they want to'.

'There's a million things to do!' said Karena, an artist and musician. 'I have a lot of concerts to give, skills to maintain and knowledge to impart. I want to see a lot more of overseas, as a performer. My partner has just started three years as a paid PhD researcher. We own no property, have a 20-year-old car and are happy as larks!'

Normajeane, 34, runs a small business with her husband, works as an artist and plays trumpet in two bands. 'I couldn't do any of that if I were stuck with a couple of children,' she wrote. 'In fact, I would argue that my life is richer and more fulfilling than [that of] any of my friends [who] have opted for a family. I know several people who have told me that they wish they had made the same decision as us but were pressured into having a family.'

The bottom line is that people are now presented with an almost limitless array of options in their lives. You could fill a dozen life spans with recreational options alone. The opportunities are even greater for people without children as their time is their own to spend.

Help the community

Volunteer work and community involvement featured strongly in the lives of the child-free people surveyed.

'We have done heaps,' said Karena, 45. 'We've helped improve our community because we have the time and energy to do so.'

G.H., 42 feels that the main thing she will leave behind is 'a lifetime of contributing to society by being involved in community activities and having been a good corporate citizen too'.

'I do voluntary work for the RSPCA and I would rather give my money to help animals,' said Stephanie, 36.

'I will continue to work as an agent for change regarding environmental awareness, devoting my energy to nurturing the planet, living with my partner in the mud brick house we built until one of us has to move into town to be closer to services,' said Ros, 45.

Lorraine, 52, plans to 'continue my involvement with our elderly neighbours, continue my involvement with the Animal Welfare League and perhaps become a WIRES carer and look after sick, orphaned or abandoned wildlife'.

The many ways in which child-free people contribute to their communities should be enough to prove wrong any claims that they are inherently selfish.

Bond with other children

Taking an active role in the lives of the children of family and friends can be a great way to satisfy a longing for the company of children. There is pleasure to be had from watching a child develop and learn, and it does not have to be your own child. Many parents will appreciate an offer of help or the ongoing interest in their child's welfare, probably because it is so rare. And best of all, you can give them back at the end of the day.

You could invite your friends' children to stay during the school holidays or organise an outing to the zoo or to a National Park. Or if you have a special skill, why not teach it to young people? Sports coaches for children's teams are always in demand, and there has been a recent boom in after-school coaching.

CHILD-FREE ZONE

'I go to efforts to ensure close relationships with a number of children – phone calls, birthdays, visits, outings, even holidays,' said Gayle, 36. 'Kids generally are fun and teach and remind us of some important values – care, concern, compassion, humility, give and take.'

'My best friend from school has three children [whom] we have adopted as "nieces" and are very close to,' said Helen, 33. 'It is great to see them and spend time with them, but also nice when they go home.'

'I really enjoy being an auntie,' said Sally, 51. 'I think I am a natural at it. I also have often felt like an honorary auntie towards the children of friends, even though I am careful not to intrude on the mothers' sphere.'

'I have strong ties to many of the children I have taught over the years,' said Anne, a high school teacher. 'As they grow into young adults, I keep in contact by phone or letter, and I'm often privy to their deepest, darkest secrets – and their joys. It's as if I have much of the joy of parenthood without the pain. I have an outlet for my beliefs and personality type through teaching. I know I've influenced many children in positive ways.'

'Most of my friends have young children, and I enjoy having them in my home and entertaining the kids more so than the parents sometimes,' said Heather, 32.

'There are many special children in my life [whom] I love, cherish, care for and spoil,' said Sue, 35. 'I look forward to seeing them and plan special events with them. I treat them as friends at all ages and enjoy their love and affection. I will also discipline them when needed, if they are in my care. Virtually all of our friends have children. Of course, I prefer it when they are in a good mood and behave well.'

It should be obvious from these comments that child-free people are generally not child haters and can have a lot to offer children –

especially time – provided their friends who are parents are happy to include them in their social circle.

Own pets

Harry the dog is an Old English Sheepdog who is now 8 years old. We bought him when we got back from our honeymoon. We decided that having a dog is a much better alternative than children. Why?

–   At the age of just 6 months, he was house trained, and by 12 months, he had passed all his obedience exams.

–   He could play cricket at 12 months old, and has had the same footy for 7 years.

–   He has never asked for Reeboks, Nintendos, Levis, or any CDs.

–   He is intact, and stands at stud (if you tried this with your children, you would be labelled a sexual monster).

–   He is happy eating dog food.

–   When we take our annual holiday, he goes off to a kennel for the duration at eight dollars a day.

–   He loves us unconditionally, and never succumbs to peer pressure.

–   If we are going out, he never needs a babysitter.

–   You can lock him out the back when you want to.

–   He has one bath a week, and only requires five hours brushing a week.

–   He'll probably die by the time he is 13 or 14 years old, and that's when kids are becoming a real problem.

- All in all, he is the perfect child, and with his feline sidekick, Jack the Bastard, makes our house the perfect family.

- If all else fails, you can shoot a bad dog...

Email sent to Triple J radio following an interview with the authors in June 1998

One of the more common stereotypes is the child-free person who lavishes love and affection on a dog or cat as if it were a child. Are pets 'child substitutes'? Our attitude on the subject is that is doesn't matter if they are, as long as the animal is wanted and well cared for. The unfortunate thing is that when people with pets have a child, the animal is often neglected. Suddenly the cat that was used to sleeping on the lounge is banished from the house and the dog is ignored or punished for playing 'too rough' with the infant. There's no time or energy for long walks anymore.

'I receive a great deal of pleasure from my furry friends who I don't think I could do without,' said Gabrielle, 32. 'If they become my surrogate children, is there anything really wrong with that?'

'Our golden retriever dogs give us enormous pleasure and much of our time is spent walking them and enjoying their company,' said Alan, 46.

It is wonderful to come home to find someone waiting for you, who loves you and is thrilled to see you. With a child, this is experienced during an all-too-short dependent phase. An animal will give you this joy for their entire lifetime.

Leave legacies

Like many other non-parents, after funding our own retirement, we will most likely leave anything left over to a charity that assists in animal care or the environment. Rather then being a 'drain' on resources as they are sometimes seen, older child-free people frequently contribute much more than others financially.

'I will be happy in the knowledge that I didn't contribute because I had to,' said Tracie, a ranger.

'I have spent most of my life treading very lightly on the earth in terms of energy consumption,' said Karena, an artist. 'I have tried, and continue to try, to enlighten people about the environment and nature and the complexity of human relationships through paintings and music. I will leave behind me paintings, books, songs, images, and hundreds of people trained in the arts.'

'At the very least, I will leave my story – that is just as important as anyone else's,'said Fiona, 41.

Where parents will almost always leave their estates to their children automatically, child-free people have to make different plans for the distribution of any money or possessions after their death.

'I will leave money for animal charities and my godchildren and that's it,' said Stephanie, 36.

'I am paying off a block of land,' said Pauline, 55. 'I don't want to make a song and dance about it, but I'm hoping that my block of land, my 100 acres, might be able to qualify for nature reserve status. That would be a binding thing, if the land were sold it would never be allowed to revert to farmland. I already applied and they said it was too degraded as cows were kept on it for some time. I also hope to leave it to local Aboriginal people. If someone could lay claim to it, I would be very happy just to leave it to them. I feel very strongly about reconciliation and I would like to think that it could be of some use to an Aboriginal group in our area.'

Marianne, 31, will leave behind 'the property I share with my partner – I can imagine part of this being kept as a reserve. Or if we sell it I would make a donation to an environmental cause that can at least continue on with something useful like a contraception program in developing countries!'

'I hope the contributions we make to environmental and animal rights charities will make a difference,' said Betty, 47. 'What we will not have left is a single bit of rubbish created by our offspring. We will not have contributed to growing landfills with our children's throwaway plastic toys, disposable nappies, mountains of paper for school work, broken bikes, obsolete computers and so on. We will not leave children whose reaching adulthood creates more demand for housing, water, food and recreation that means further destruction of untouched wilderness areas.'

'Having had careers as a nurse, midwife and parenting educator – including four years teaching childbirth education – ironic? – I feel I've done my bit for society,' said Lyndall, 47. 'I had a mission to make the first days of motherhood easier for women. I now work in community adult education so am still in a "socially responsible" environment.'

'My partner and I talk about auctioning off our belongings, taking what we need to survive and leaving the rest to charity,' said Beth. 'I don't have any driving need for people to know it was me who helped. I just hope when it happens that I am happy with the way I have lived my life. If it happened tomorrow I wouldn't think I had missed out on anything.'

Build a child-free network

The difficulties of maintaining friendships with parents makes it necessary to seek out the company of other like-minded people. Some do this from necessity as their circle of friends dwindles, while others don't like to be in the company of children. They avoid kids by finding friends in the same situation.

'We have tended to gravitate towards other people without children, just like parents prefer to talk to other parents,' said Sarah, 39. 'Luckily in our industry, there are many others like us and we have formed a social group. Our circle of friends includes older people whose children are now adults.'

'We do have a network of child-free friends,' said Laura, a 41-year-old doctor. 'We have tentative plans to buy a large house and subdivide it into independent units with some common living areas so that we can care for each other in our old age and employ a helper as required.'

Child-free couples often challenge the idea of family and community. Is a household without children a 'family'? We certainly think so, and with so many Australian households comprising just two people it should have a broader interpretation. Yet so called 'family policy' is about families with children.

'This is a small community and we watch out for each other – this includes little people as well as big ones,' said Karena, who lives in a small coastal town. 'I teach art, film making and festival production to young and older people and I'm an integral part of our extended family.'

Study and explore personal interests

Child-free people generally have more spare time and fewer distractions at home which allows them to participate in further study and explore personal interests.

Jan, 57, says she will probably work until it is 'no longer an option. I have completed several university degrees, which has given me the opportunity to be flexible in my work environment. I will probably do more "interest courses" in the future'.

Janelle, 33, says she will spend the rest of her life 'basically taking up all the challenges the world has to offer. I will be able to consider any opportunities that come my way, being financially independent, travelling, studying and developing my career into my lifestyle.'

As people without children cannot transfer their ambitions to their offspring, they have to take it upon themselves to do the best they possibly can and achieve what they hope for. No one else is going to do it for them.

Travel and take risks

Freedom to travel was a recurring theme in most of the questionnaires we received. For many child-free people, travel, adventure and risk taking are a way of life.

A study conducted in the UK by the Family Policy Studies Centre, and reported in a British newspaper article sent to us by a child-free relative, found that people who choose to be childless are not radical, but rather deeply conservative and fearful of risk taking. Those in the study were considered 'risk averse' for shunning parenthood, largely because of the seriousness of the undertaking.

In reality, it depends a lot on what a person considers to be a high risk activity. Having a child when there are no guarantees on how it will grow up is certainly a great risk. Leaving a steady job to start a small business or work as an artist, pulling up roots to live and work overseas, jumping from a plane or working as a volunteer in a Third World country are also 'risky' activities.

A friend of ours was forced to sell his much loved motorbike when his first child was born. The risk was simply too great, his wife told him, and he could not have another one until the child turned 18. Then she had a second child, then a third, and the date when he could relive the joy that bike riding gave him moved further away. He's since got into motor racing instead, and *tries* to hide the various modifications he has done on the car from his wife.

'My life's mission is to spend as much time as I can with my wife travelling the world, experiencing what it has to offer to the fullest,' said John, 37. 'I seek stimulation from employment too, and companionship and devotion to the success of my marriage.'

Parents often claim that their children 'keep them young'. They mean that they have retained a 'younger' attitude from being around young people. Child-free people can also keep a young outlook on life by being open to all that the world has to offer.

Child-free zones

Most child-free people do not go out of their way to avoid contact with children. However, most appreciate the opportunity to enjoy adult company without them. As Fiona, 32, put it: 'We avoid family restaurants and G rated films – though we both love a good toyshop.'

'I avoid situations where I might encounter [children], for example picnic grounds or holiday venues outside school terms,' said Kate, 55.

Last year we were looking forward to treating Mum to a nice birthday lunch at a beachside restaurant with a reputation for excellent food. We were seated at a table for three in the centre of the restaurant, surrounded by large tables, each with a small child or baby in a carrier. Each of them screamed throughout our lunch and totally ruined the experience. Parents will talk of the need to be tolerant and understanding, while non-parents may feel that their needs and feelings are disregarded. It is considered poor form to complain about the poor behaviour of children or their parents.

'I think that a lot of parents are very inconsiderate when it comes to taking their children out in public places,' said Normajeane, 34. 'They should think about where they're taking the kids and how their behaviour can affect other people. I don't want to listen to a screaming child when I'm at a nice restaurant, at an art exhibition, watching a movie or when I'm at band practice. Small children playing chasey around expensive musical instruments is a recipe for disaster and yet it seems politically incorrect to say anything.'

Public places such as restaurants cannot advertise themselves as 'child-free' and not allow children, probably due to anti-discrimination laws. Lynch's Restaurant of Melbourne caused a stir when it displayed a sign in the window saying that babies were not allowed. A couple took them to court over the issue and they made prime time news with their child-free stand. The result could not be technically called a win for Lynch's as discrimination was found to have occurred. However, Lynch's didn't have to pay any court costs and didn't have to alter their policy. They were advised to put a sign in the front window indicating that they reserved the right to refuse service to people under the age of 12. Lynch's told us that they received over 400 letters of support, endless congratulatory phone calls and only two letters that were opposed to their stance. One of our survey respondents kindly sent us a postcard from Lynch's that features a cartoon of a screaming baby and the words 'Baby Free Zone' on the front.

The manager of a tourist facility in the Hunter Valley region of New South Wales wrote that they simply note on all promotional literature that they have 'no facilities for children'. She says that during the school holidays, they are always fully booked with schoolteachers. 'Word has got around that we offer adult accommodation, and it is greatly appreciated by all our guests. This is not easy to do – in fact I am technically breaking the law, so I have to be Very Careful with my bookings.'

Some of the more exclusive Barrier Reef island resorts cater specifically for couples and make it clear that they do not cater for children under 16. An increasing number of bed and breakfast style guesthouses do the same.

As some of our survey respondents pointed out, there are ways to enjoy activities without the interference of misbehaving children. After all, when you are there you don't have a choice in the behaviour of the children who also happen to be there. It is easiest to avoid all of them.

We have learnt to not even contemplate taking holidays during school holidays. This has an added bonus of being cheaper than peak times and the roads are considerably safer with less traffic.

The flexibility of child-free travel, both internationally and domestically, can provide considerable savings for a variety of reasons. Recently we visited Disney World in Orlando, Florida. This destination may sound like a total mistake for the child-free, child-avoiding couple. After all, these places are made for kids. Despite this we were determined to satisfy the children within us.

We visited the park in the off-peak season so crowds were at a minimum. When we went to the theme parks we went very early in the morning, before most families could get organised, or late at night when most families were worn out. We managed to avoid queuing for all but one major attraction. It was amazing.

We exhausted one theme park per day. Families we spoke to were on their third and fourth visits to a single park, and told us that they needed that many visits to cater for the slower progress made by larger family groups.

We were also able to apply some strategy to our visit. We knew that we were only there for a short time so we pushed the sleep envelope. We did everything we could all day every day, planning to do our catch-up sleeping on the way home in the plane. You can't do this with kids. When they get sleepy and whiney there is nothing you can do but let them rest.

Another simple strategy we have is to avoid 'family' restaurants where possible. Not only is this label an indicator that vast numbers of children will be present, but it also tends to be a flag as to the quality of the meals available.

There are coach trips and cruises that advertise themselves as catering for adults. We suspect this is to do with the licensing laws and free availability of alcohol more than the intention of catering for adults who don't want to interact with children. If the world is your pub then everyone has to be of drinking age.

Often our stamina alone eventually provides us with the sort of child-free experience that we appreciate in public places. For example, most parents with children will leave a restaurant well before we need to.

The true 'child-free zone' is very rare. Many adults are far more childish than children, and not in a particularly flattering way either. Many of our survey respondents have pointed out to us by that they are happy to interact with well behaved children, just as they prefer to interact with well behaved adults. It is fine to choose who your adult friends are, but when you try to choose your children friends you are in big trouble. You have to love them all!

We'd like to provide a list of child-free facilities, restaurants, activities, organisations, clubs and holidays, but few of these facilities are advertised as such in guides or brochures. Many generate awareness through word of mouth.

If you have some information that may be of benefit to child-free people in this regard, please contact us via any of the methods outlined in the back of this book. We are happy to collect this information and use it for future revisions of this book or put it on our web site.

Our story

Having read the many wonderful personal stories dispersed throughout the book, we thought that by now you may be wondering what our story is and what prompted us to choose this path. This certainly has been a favourite question of the media.

Susan's story

Age 30

As an only child, I didn't grow up around many other kids. Dad's family is in England and most of Mum's family lives in Newcastle, north of Sydney, a three hour drive away in those days. I've never spent much time with children, especially babies, and as a result I don't feel comfortable around them. I don't know what to do with them, I don't enjoy their company and I refuse to talk 'baby language' to them. Even as a kid I generally preferred the company of older children and adults. This hasn't changed and I don't remember a single 'maternal moment'.

In my late teens I had a vivid dream that I'd met the man of my dreams. Then the handsome, charming guy declared that he wanted six children, and I remember running as fast as I could towards the horizon. As a schoolgirl I decided that I would never get married and have kids. I saw the two as inextricably entwined. Most of my family and friends also thought I'd never get married. In my school yearbook I listed my ambition as 'to have a house in the suburbs, a dog, two kids, a mother-in-law and a Ford (or as few from that as possible)'. Funniest thing is, I've now had everything on that list at some time except the kids!

I don't think my Mum ever planned to have children either. But once she was pregnant with me she decided she did want a child. She was a wonderful mum and is really good with babies, but as she grows older, she too has little tolerance for small children. Like me, she likes a certain amount of order and control in her life. So luckily grandchildren are not a big priority for her, or for Dad, who doesn't have patience with kids either. He doesn't understand 'cute' – neither do I.

Mum and Dad sacrificed a lot for the good education and the varied experiences I had growing up. I'm sure they would think I had 'wasted' it if I stayed home and had kids. I think they envisioned a jet-setting executive daughter in a high-flying career. I'm not quite that, but I think they would be disappointed if I became a mum. They were surprised enough when I got married.

I'm not afraid of childbirth but terrified of post-natal depression. I'm certain that if I were alone at home with a baby one or both of us would suffer. I sometimes think it would be the kid or me – one of us would have to go. And as I can't bear to think of people hurting kids, I can't risk putting myself in that situation. A few years ago I had nose surgery and during the two weeks I was home from work with a bandaged nose, we bought our first cat. I'm a big cat lover and, as cute as she was, a couple of days being stuck at home with the endless mewing and I was ready to kill her. I could almost have picked up the tiny kitten and hurled it through the window. A crying baby would be far worse.

There are so many things I want to do in my life that I just don't see how I'd fit a child in. Like many people, I want to pay off my home, build a career and have the flexibility to change career paths, travel more and save enough to fund my own comfortable retirement. I want to spend quality time with my husband, learn another language or two, read more, draw, cook, write to friends and keep in touch with family. I'd like to learn to sing, keep fit, volunteer my time to help animals and people and most of all, keep on learning until the day I die. As it is I'll have a hard time fitting it all in.

Recently a lot of my friends and colleagues have started families and I can see I'll have increasing contact with kids over the next ten years. I was quite fond of one colleague's small son, in particular; I was fascinated by his language abilities. But seeing them struggle with money and day care and health crises doesn't make me any more attracted to having children. I think some of my friends will make great parents. It's just not for me. That's my choice and I'd like others to accept it. I think many of them will envy me for it some day.

David's story

Age 33

As *Child-Free Zone* progressed, each new opinion and every new reason that crossed our desk seemed to be part of my own reasons for choosing to be child-free. Not many of the reasons were new to me, but when they were I assimilated them into my own. I have learnt the hard way to 'never say never', but at this stage in my life I am as confident as I can be that I will never have children by choice.

I don't remember the point in time when this realisation came about. I just remember thinking that I didn't really enjoy my childhood and I wouldn't want to put another child through that. I remember many of the negative emotions I had, and the horrible things that I did to my parents while I was 'just being a kid'. I decided I did not want to be on the receiving end of those things.

I have a bad temper, but I am a small person. Early on I learnt that my temper alone was going to get me into trouble. However, a child of mine would be smaller than me for some time. I am not confident enough in my emotional control to guarantee that I would not end up in jail after throwing my screaming child through a window. I would care too much about the child and myself to risk experiencing either of those things.

My father once said to me, 'I want you to have kids so you can suffer the way I have.' Though I suspect it was as much in jest as in seriousness. My brother and I weren't bad kids, but we weren't good kids either. I can say without a hint of ego that my parents were lucky. I realised that there were no guarantees in raising children and if I was going to take notice of anything my father said, this one back-handed piece of wisdom seemed a good thing to choose.

I hated school from the day I walked in to the day I walked out. I do not want to put anybody I am responsible for through that. But if you have kids, you have to send them to school.

Everywhere I turned I saw double standards and hypocrisy involved in parenting: 'do as I say, not as I do'. I didn't like that then and I still don't like it now. 'If you can't be honest with your children and explain to them why things are the way they are...' But then as a parent you get tired of explaining everything.

As I grew up and started working I came to realise that money was hard to come by and that you needed a damn lot of it to get by in life. It wasn't long before a couple of bad relationships with greedy women made me realise that I wasn't going to pay for anybody's free ride on this planet and this included any children that I may have had with them – hypothetically speaking of course.

After a while I grew to generally dislike children. It seemed like every one of them I encountered was obnoxious, naughty, whiney, precocious, noisy, lying, manipulating, annoying, disobedient and misbehaved. And I just did not want to deal with it. I certainly did not want a child like this of my own. The behaviour of these children and their parents was making me somebody I did not want to be. I had to fake interest and enjoyment. I had to force conversations with toddlers and parents alike. I had to comfort childhood traumas induced by *nothing* that would disappear mysteriously in a moment. Life is too short and I did not want to be false with my friends and their children. My public child-free stance has allowed me to be honest with these people and that is a good thing.

Honesty and fairness are things that I value deeply. My Tae Kwon Do instructor once quoted to me 'people do not have to earn my respect, they just have to lose it'. Children seem to be able to lie and deceive especially easily, with little or no guilt, thus losing my respect. They also do it repeatedly without repercussions. They are just undisciplined and the law won't let parents discipline them any more. I think it is a good thing that I would want to raise a child who would be disciplined and socially acceptable. I just don't think I can.

I loathe over-packaging and disposable things irritate me enormously. Misused resources and misguided spending make me fear for the human race. I feel especially sad for the animal victims of man's activity. I would prefer that my taxes were spent on saving an endangered species rather than accelerating the human plague. I don't want to cause any more environmental problems than I have to and I certainly don't want to add another consumer to this over-burdened planet. Certainly not one who *could* turn out to be a worse global citizen than I am.

Despite all the benefits of not having a child, the bottom line is that I care so much that I refuse to take the risk of giving my child a bad life. For me the risks are greater than for most people. In many ways I have been lucky in life and I have been clever too. I strongly believe that this combination has led me to realise that having a child is not right *for me*. I wish more people this good fortune.

Susan J. & David L. Moore

You aren't on your own

Up until now you may have thought you were on your own, among a freak group of like-minded friends, or just plain weird. 'I thought I was the only one!', 'My friends all think I am weird and I'll change my mind', 'My girlfriends all think the same way but are being pressured to have kids', and so it goes on.

So many people are now choosing to stay child-free that it's surprising that it's even an issue.

The more we get out and about the more we see and hear child-free things that we wouldn't have noticed as little as two years ago. It would be lovely to think that we had already made an impact. But the truth is that a lot of people are realising this on their own and slowly connecting with other like-minded people.

During the writing of this book we have appeared on television, radio and in various forms of the print media. Each time we were approached out of the blue as a result of a previous appearance in one media or another. We have not actively sought the publicity we have received. People are interested and they are listening. Awareness is growing and it is now our turn to speak.

When we started this book we were mostly doing it to connect the supporters and increase the understanding of the ignorant or the non-supporters. Each time we appeared on radio or TV we prepared ourselves for an attack. We prepared for the worst case scenario and we expected to battle for our opinion to be heard. We thought we were there as a curiosity and that afterwards the audience would forget about our opinion like last year's hoola hoop. To our surprise we were not attacked, we did not have to fight to be heard, and we weren't a passing fad. The people that were involved and responded to those shows were overwhelmingly supportive, encouraging and friendly. Even people with families were apparently understanding of our point of view and did not take it as a personal affront.

CHILD-FREE ZONE

We're not saying that no one should have children. What we *are* saying is that everybody should think about it before they decide. Some people should have children, some people shouldn't. The boundaries are always going to be blurred and the correct choice clearer with hindsight.

We like to think that we have included the experience of others in our child-free decision. Life is short and you can't always 'suck it and see'. Listen to other people's opinions but assess the facts for yourself and do the right thing for you.

It is fine to change your mind too. If the factors affecting your original decision no longer apply that is fine. For many child-free people there are simply too many clear cut reasons and the decision is not worth revisiting. For some it is a matter of circumstance and, if the obstacles could be cleared, the choice may be different in the future. For still more people the decision may be too late, but at least understanding it in hindsight can help you to deal with the problems you may be experiencing now.

Ultimately, to not have children is a valid decision — the keyword being *decision*. The choice should be accepted and respected. It's certainly not *bad* to have children, but it can be *great* not to.

Life is very complex and more often than not well out of our control. Your future circumstances may end up nullifying your decision, whatever it may be. There is no point in worrying about what may be; there are plenty of reasons to think positively, work with what you've got (and towards what you want), and not to second guess a well made decision.

Until recently, the child-free voice has not been heard. We're sure we'll offend some people along the way, but we are now going to be heard and people are going to hear the truth about the child-free alternative.

Good luck to you and we hope you have a wonderful child-free future!

Participate in our survey

We have included our survey in case you'd like to know what questions prompted the responses in the book.

Many people have also indicated that they wanted to use it as a self-evaluation exercise or perhaps compare it to their partner's responses. You can also fill it in and send it back to us. Future revisions will include additional material that has been prompted by this book. We're especially looking for responses that raise some new issues not found in the book already.

Questionnaire for child-free people

Your first name _____
(please use a pseudonym if you do not wish your name to be used)

Are you: ❐   Male   ❐
         Female

Your age _____

Are you: ❐   Married   ❐
         Single
              ❐   Living de facto   ❐
         Divorced
              ❐   Widowed

Are you: ❐   Heterosexual
              ❐   Gay or lesbian
              ❐   Other _____

Your occupation:

_____

_____

Your highest level of education:

              ❐   School – year 10/form 4
              ❐   School – year 12/Form 6
              ❐   Undergraduate degree
              ❐   Postgraduate degree

☐   College or TAFE

☐   Other _____

How many brothers or sisters do you have? ____

When did you decide not to have children? Was there a circumstance that prompted this?

_____
_____
_____
_____
_____
_____
_____
_____

Was it a personal decision only or a joint decision with a partner?

_____
_____
_____
_____
_____

If you are in a relationship, does one of you want children less than the other?

☐   Yes   ☐   No

Does this cause strains in your relationship?

_____

_____

_____

_____

_____

_____

What are your three main reasons for choosing not to
have a child?

1._____

_____

_____

2._____

_____

_____

3._____

_____

_____

What do you see as the main benefit of being child-free?

_____

_____

_____

_____

_____

_____

What do you believe to be the negatives to being child-free?

_____

_____

_____

_____

_____

_____

_____

_____

Have you felt pressured to have a family? If so, how?

_____

_____

_____

_____

_____

_____

_____

_____

CHILD-FREE ZONE

How do you feel towards the children of family and friends?

_____

_____

_____

_____

_____

_____

_____

_____

How do you feel towards the children of strangers?

_____

_____

_____

_____

_____

_____

_____

_____

What form of contraception do you and/or your partner currently use?

_____

_____

_____

_____

_____

How would an unplanned pregnancy affect your decision
to remain child-free?

_____

_____

_____

_____

_____

_____

_____

_____

_____

Have you or would you consider being sterilised? If you
have, please provide details.

_____

_____

_____

_____

_____

_____

_____

_____

What effect do you think remaining child-free has on your career or work?

_____

_____

_____

_____

_____

_____

_____

_____

_____

_____

Have you discussed your decision with friends or family?

❒　　Yes　　　　❒　　No

Why, or why not?

_____

_____

_____

_____

_____

_____

_____

_____

What reaction have you had from those you have told?

_____

_____

_____

_____

_____

_____

_____

Is this a definite decision? What would make you change your mind?

_____

_____

_____

_____

_____

_____

_____

How have global factors such as environmental issues, population issues, political and economic unrest or war affected your decision?

_____

_____

_____

_____

_____

_____

How do you imagine that having a child would affect your life?

_____

_____

_____

_____

_____

_____

_____

_____

How do you foresee spending the rest of your life?

_____

_____

_____

_____

_____

_____

_____

_____

If you die childless, what will you leave the world when you are gone?

_____

_____

_____

_____

_____

_____

_____

Do you (or do you think you will ever) regret your decision?

_____

_____

_____

_____

_____

_____

_____

_____

If you would agree to being interviewed further, please provide contact details:

Full name:

_____

Address:

_____

_____

_____

_____

Phone number
    (daytime): _____
    (evening): _____

How to contact us

You can contact us via the following channels.

    Susan J. & David L. Moore
2 Larmer Place
Dee Why NSW 2099
Australia
Ph: +612 9981 7636
Fax: +612 9984 0144
Web site: www.childfree.com.au
Email: authors@childfree.com.au

Thanks for your time and interest.

References

Australian Bureau of Statistics, *Year Book Australia 1997*.

Bartlett, Jane, *Will You Be Mother? Women who choose to say no*, Virago Press, London, 1997.

Biggins, Felicity, 'Try the view from the front, suckers', *The Australian*, 30 January 1996.

Bita, Natasha, 'Couples choose careers over children', *The Australian*, 2 October 1998.

Clark, Dr David, 'Rethinking our Robin Hood taxes', Economic briefing in *Australian Financial Review*, 5 June 1996.

Coppell, Bill, *Australia in Facts and Figures*, Penguin Books Australia, 1994.

Dargan, Felicity, 'Mixed blessing' in *Sunday Herald-Sun*, 29 March 1998.

Faludi, Susan, *Backlash: The undeclared war against American women*, Crown, New York, 1991.

Gittins, Ross, 'Children – they're just priceless', *Sydney Morning Herald*, 15 September 1999.

Gora, Bronwen, 'High cost of raising kids', © *The Sunday Telegraph*, 19 April 1998.

Hulme, Jenny, 'Married, Without Children', *New Woman*, January 1995.

Jeffers, Susan, *I'm Okay, You're a Brat*, Hodder Headline Australia, Sydney, 1999.

Susan J. & David L. Moore

Johnson, Cathy, 'No kids no worries', *Sydney Morning Herald*, 7 July 1990.

Lewis, Berwyn, *No Children by Choice*, Penguin Books Australia, 1986.

Mackay, Hugh, *Reinventing Australia – the mind and mood of Australia in the 1990s*, Collins Angus & Robertson, 1993.

Macken, Deirdre, 'Do I make you angry, baby?', *Australian Financial Review*, 14 August 1999.

Mackinnon, Alison, *Love and Freedom – Professional women and the reshaping of personal life*, Cambridge University Press, UK, 1997.

Marshall, Helen, *Not Having Children*, Oxford University Press Australia, 1993.

Maushart, Susan, *The Mask of Motherhood*, Vintage Australia, Random House, 1997.

McDonald, Peter, *Families in Australia: A socio-demographic perspective*, Australian Institute of Family Studies, Melbourne, 1995.

O'Rourke, P.J., *All the trouble in the world*, Pan Macmillan, 1994.

Patty, Anna, 'Dads get the blues too', *The Sun Herald*, 13 December 1998.

Safer, Jeanne, *Beyond Motherhood – Choosing a life without children*, Pocket Books (Simon & Schuster), New York, 1996.

Weiss, Donald H., 'Making tough decisions', American Management Association, New York, 1993.

Index

About the authors

David and Susan Moore knew by their early twenties that they did not want to have children, and were lucky enough to find a like-minded partner. They met at work in 1992 and married less than twelve months later. Now in their early thirties and living in Dee Why on Sydney's northern beaches, they wonder how they would ever find time to be parents.

David is an independent software testing consultant and front man of Sydney ska band Dr Raju. He has a black belt in Tae Kwon Do, is learning to play the trumpet and trains at the gym. Susan is a public relations consultant with a Bachelor of Arts in Communication from Charles Sturt University in Bathurst. After years of ballet classes, Susan is now learning to tap dance, improving her German and going to the gym. She is only slightly obsessive about cats. Both are active members of a car club and Zoo Friends, and enjoy taking the Ducati out on weekends.

Merchandise

An ever changing array of merchandise, both humorous and serious, is available through our web site:

> www.childfree.com.au

and our CafePress sites:

> www.cafepress.com/cfz

> www.cafepress.com/childfreesigns

> www.cafepress.com/boredwithbabies

Also by D.L. Moore

Complain and Win – your guide to consumer justice.

Available through CafePress at:

> www.cafepress.com/complainandwin

9564398R0

Made in the USA
Lexington, KY
09 May 2011